Budgetary Thought for School Officials

A Budgetmaker's Perspective

Edward Anthony Lehan

Frist Edition © 1982 Edward Anthony Lehan
Revised Edition © 2019 Edward Anthony Lehan

Edward Anthony Lehan
89 Rumford Street
West Hartford, CT 06107
(860) 521-7097
ealehan@att.net

ISBN: 978-1-4566-3500-8

Books and Monographs by the Author

The Practice of Municipal Budgeting - A Self-Instruction Text (Bureau of Governmental Research, University of Rhode Island, 1975.)

Simplified Governmental Budgeting. (Governmental Finance Officers Association, 1981)

Budgetary Thought for School Officials, (First Edition,. (Cantabrigia, 1982.)

Budgetmaking – A Workbook of Public Budgeting Theory and Practice (St. Martins Press, 1964.)

Budgetary Thought for Budget Officers – A Practitioner's Perspective. (Amazon, 2015.)

Managerial Thought for Public Finance Officers – A Practitioner's Perspective (Amazon, 2016.)

Public Budgeting (Institute of Public Service, University of Connecticut, 1967)

Rebuilding a City: Modest Adventures in Hartford "Public Management" (International City managers Association, 1968.) Louis Brownlow Award, 1968

Various articles on finance "Governmental Finance." Governmental Finance Officers Association, 1976&1979

Determinants of Local Government Capability (Institute of Public Service, University of Connecticut, 1978)

The Future of the Finance Directorate (Municipal Finance Officers Association, Study #3, 1/2/78)

Organization of the Finance Function, **Local Government Finance,** (Government Finance Officers Association, Chapter 3, pp. 29-43, 1991)

Budget Appraisal: The Next Step in Budget Betterment? "Public Budgeing and Finance," 1996. Jesse Burkhead Award.

Contents

First Edition Preface

If I could have my way, this slender volume would be required reading for all educators, especially those who lead the public schools.

I became acquainted with Mr. Lehan's work during my tenure as a member and president of the School Board of Rochester, New York. As a result, I moved with much greater personal assurance on budget issues, and, most importantly, I was emboldened to encourage and support a thorough transformation of our budget practices.

As its title proclaims, this is an essay about the intellectual foundations of budgeting. With remorseless logic, it expounds a proposition that budgetmaking should be a thought process about the worth of things, not an exercise in the price of things. With great clarity, and vigorous prose, this essay drives home the point that budgets are better understood, and, thus, more efficacious, if formulated, debated and adopted in terms of formal allocation criteria, such as, unit cost, unit times, investment returns, and marginal productivity.

Budgetary Thought for School Officials is a workbook. It is peppered with illustrations and exercises which encourage budgetmakers to develop flexible classification schemes, performance data arrays, and budget formulations in an "issue paper" format. This book says precious little about traditional budgetary concerns, such as accounting or control. It does not even dwell on expenditures, as one might expect in a book about budgeting. It is, rather, a book about mental qualities and methodical work, done to exacting standards. That's why this book is so refreshing, so illuminating, and, ultimately, so useful. No educator should be without it!

Josephine Genovese
Rochester, New York
Summer, 1981

Acknowledgements

The School District of Rochester, New York, began an ambitious budget improvement project in the fall of 1980. It was my on-the-job experiences as an advisor that inspired me to compose the first edition of *Budgetary Thought for School Officials*.

The first year's effort expanded staff and parent participation, developed objective allocation criteria, produced a balanced 1981-82 budget, down 10 percent, and provided an array of program options for School Board consideration. The revamped procedures helped to attract community support for School Board decisions on program reductions and school closings. The second year's effort featured, 1) a three-year financial plan embracing program options and collective bargaining scenarios, 2) an extensive assembly of data useful in relating expenditures and revenues to student performance, and 3) a further expansion of staff participation. To be associated with this innovative project was a rare privilege.

I gratefully acknowledge the contribution of the then School Board, who initiated and supported systemic changes in District procedures: Archie Curry, John Delvecchio, Irene Frusci, Josephine Genovese, Karen Grella, Gary Smith, and Frank Willis.

Proving their mettle as first-class budget craftsmen, Peter McWalters, Director of Planning and Resource Allocation, and Michael Robinson, Executive Assistant to the Superintendent, contributed more than they know to the form and substance of the first edition. I am especially grateful to Superintendent Laval Wilson, who merited high praise for his willingness to experiment and persevere. His leadership and skill endowed the budget improvement project with the essential ingredients of unity, energy and duration. In composing this revised, expanded edition, I am deeply indebted to reviewers Marie Brandt, Luke Williams, and the ever-diligent. Joseph T. Kelley.

Edward Anthony Lehan
West Hartford, CT, April 30, 2020

To the Reader

To budget well is to practice a craft. This thesis may startle those school officials who have concluded that budgetmaking is neither art nor craft, but "politics," pure and simple. School officials of this persuasion see budgetmaking as an arbitrary exercise, requiring the manipulative talents of propagandists, partisans and special pleaders, rather than the straight-forward skills of craftsmen. Why bother with evidence and logic, they say, when "push, pull and pressure" rule the budgetary process? If you believe in the political theory of budgeting, this essay is not for you. If, on the other hand, you see an enhanced role for evidence and logic in the budgetary process, and you wish to improve the quality of your thinking and action, the recommendations of this essay can help.

As noted by my acknowledgements, I composed the first edition to codify my consulting experience with the School District of Rochester, New York. By publishing it as a workbook, I hoped to direct attention to the conceptions and supporting practices that I had recommended. Over the years since, observing the increasing public concern about the performance of public education, and the attempts at remedies, I feel that my recommended conceptions and supporting practice are as relevant today as they were in 1981, perhaps, even more so. Since 1981, I have had additional experiences, testing my conceptions of efficacious budgetary thought and action. Taking form as an expository essay, rather than a workbook, this revised edition is the result.

There is no shortage of budgetary literature. The focus of this literature, however, is institutional, rather than personal. Ironically, even the "how-to-do-it" books tend to present budgetmaking as an organizational process, treating procedures and techniques as disembodied abstractions. Reflecting my teaching and consulting experience, flesh and blood budgetmakers, wrestling with the dilemmas of resource allocation, do not find this literature of significant assistance. Consequently, I did not want *Budgetary Thought for School Officials* to be just another book *about* budgeting, although one can obviously learn much about budgetary processes from a study of its pages. Rather, this essay is about "intellectual furniture" that is, mental dispositions that can help accountable educators to make efficacious allocations of scarce resources among competing educational purposes. *As an ideal, budgetmaking should be a thought process about the worth of things, rather than solely an exercise in the price of things.* Thus, this essay has a lofty aim: assist educators to acquire those qualities of mind, and a willingness to practice that enhance their competence in executing this critical task.

Following a recommended pedagogical practice (see my reference to the **SQ3R** Method below), the reader would do well to convert the title of this essay into a provocative question: What, exactly, is budgetary thought? I believe that an active search for an adequate answer to this question will help determine the usefulness of my essay to the reader. As the reader will discover, I define budgetary thought as specialized thinking about rationing scarce resources, occurring in situations where desires are strongly conditioned by constraints.

> *The necessity to ration scarce resources among competing purposes is the cause and consequence of budgetary thinking.*

Rooted in the reality of rationing, every commitment of funds forecloses other possible budget allocations. Foreclosure is the "opportunity cost" of a decision. Every "yes" is simultaneously a "no." When rationing resources, the budgetary effectiveness of educators depends on their ability to think appropriately in terms of this, the reality of their action. Again, referencing the ideal cited above, budgetmaking should be a thought process about the worth of things, as well as consideration of the price of things. With this ideal in view, the reader should proceed to frame the question in specific terms: What is budgetary thought when applied by educators to education? This essay is my response to this key question. It advances a cohesive set of concepts which can assist school authorities, and the accountable staff, to think through rationing issues, problems and opportunities to propose, adopt and implement efficacious allocations.

Regarding the socio-political background of this essay, it is fair to say that public education is as controversial today as it was during the 19th Century struggle to establish the common schools, based on compulsory attendance. For decades, the news media have been reporting data and concerns about student under-achievement and under-attainment   Reportedly, high school principals are dismayed by the poor performance of many elementary school graduates. In turn, college presidents are reportedly dismayed by the poor performance of many high school graduates. Taxpaying citizens, especially those who are parents of public school students, expect positive correlations between expenditures and indicators of student achievement and attainment. Persistent negative results cast doubt on both the quality of instruction and the wisdom of budgetary decisions. In many educational environments, traditional organizational arrangements and teaching methods appear to have lost, or are losing, their bite. Further, a sequence of attempted reforms has produced indifferent results. Vast sum have been appropriated and spent.   Meanwhile, thousands of students are being short-changed by misallocations and weak program implementation.

Gripped by adherence to traditional classroom and curriculum dynamics, elementary and secondary teachers and students live in time-sensitive environments. If lessons are not well taught, and well absorbed, at the appropriate time, and in logical sequence, subsequent acquisition of knowledge and skill is problematical.   Mastery of school-required skills must be acquired, and proven, as a condition of promotion to higher grades – a rule often ignored! (It is truly said that today's poorly performing fourth grade student is tomorrow's high school "dropout.")

Time-on-task is the precious critical variable of education. The time devoted to instruction, drill and practice counts, and counts heavily in producing student achievement.   Myriad distractions eat away the time allocated by lesson plans to instruction, drill and practice. (I dare say that this erosion of time-on-task is the key hidden waste of appropriated funds.)   Making lesson plans effective in the struggle against distractions, requires relentless monitoring and follow-up by supervisors.

7

Where entrenched the reflexive acceptance of educational conventions, such as, class size limitations and teacher pay plans based on educational attainments and time-in-service, have significant budgetary consequences. Borrowing a concept from physics, existing institutional arrangements are endowed with "inertia." Where deference to conventional arrangements prevails, budget formulation degenerates into a series of calculations to determine the cost of current practice.

> *In sharp contrast to conventional arrangements, this essay recommends the practice of solution-centered, results-oriented budgeting, supported by 1) data-driven decision-making, 2) management accounting, and 3) dynamic monitoring. When proficiently applied, this ensemble of techniques increases the likelihood that evidence and logic, rather than subjective judgment and reflexive acceptance of conventional procedure, will infuse the allocation process.*

Designed to inspire and embolden, this essay expresses my intent to incline the thinking of educators along lines of inquiry and action that will result in efficacious budgets, that is, budgets that are sharply focused on the key task of shifting the "bell curve" of student achievement right-ward. In other words, enabling pedagogy to trump sociology, and other limiting environmental influences.

Whether acknowledged, or not, science-driven technological change has been altering the environment of educational institutions. Specifically, the impact of science-driven technology *alters the way students learn, and what and when they learn.* This change challenges the way schools are organized and teachers teach. Although the tempo of responses to this change has quickened in recent years, educational authorities, in general, have reacted conservatively to the challenge.

Despite an expansion of educational usage of electronic technologies, countless millions of students find that education involves schoolhouses and classrooms, students grouped by age or interest, teacher's telling and questioning, upraised hands and chalkboard demonstrations. As pointed out by a growing legion of critics, this reliance on traditional educational practice (and its assumption of uniformity, or at least, a "normal" distribution of student capabilities in the classroom) is producing unsatisfactory results.

Influenced by Johann Pestalozzi's experiments with teaching based on child development, circa 1800, educational authorities have relied on chronological age as the basic organizing principle of elementary and secondary education. Keyed to this organic principle, standardized teaching was the best way to transfer organized knowledge and skill from adults to the young. The cumulative impact of television on the mentality of generations of children, the now ubiquitous availability of computerized information and the steady advance of educational software weaken the correlation of "learning readiness" with chronological age. Additionally, these technologies undermine the role of the teacher as the student's prime source of knowledge and skill. The educational impact of electronic media is undermining the key assumption of traditional education, and this trend will undoubtedly continue.   Increasingly, teachers are working with students differentiated by their already acquired knowledge and skill, requiring flexible rather than standardized approaches to curriculum design and instruction. In this scenario, one can foresee increasing reliance on teachers as diagnosticians, counselors and prescribers, and decreasing reliance on teachers as prime transmitters of knowledge and skill.

It is not surprising that the response of accountable officials to the manifest problems of educational ineffectiveness relies on academic and institutional solutions, including higher achievement and attainment standards, school choice and charter schools. Representing the most radical response, an increasing number of parents are reported to be withdrawing their children from schools altogether, opting for home schooling. These "solutions" do not directly address the problem of student performance. A more direct approach, as herein recommended, would

provide educators, institution by institution, with decision-making machinery and implementation instruments that can help them focus scarce resources on variables proven most likely to enhance student performance.

To attain and sustain such data-driven leadership and teaching throughout America's public schools, educational authorities should

adopt decision-making machinery and implementation instruments that integrate a) decision-related research and procedures, especially mathematical modeling, b) management accounting, and, c) solution-centered, results-oriented budgeting.

This proposed integrated approach will permit, and encourage, educators to 1) assess the impact of selected variables thought to influence student performance, and 2) use the resulting information to efficaciously allocate resources to enhance the impact of the most efficacious variables. For details on this key recommendation, see Part 3, *Administrative and Accounting Foundations,*

Craft Ideals

The first sentence of this essay was calculated to arouse your curiosity. Read it again! Then ponder this question: Why am I troubling to compare budgeting work with the work of artisans? My reasoning follows:

First, the craft concept gives us grounds for an attack on the all too popular notion that the "appropriations game" can only be won by using political arts. This corrosive notion is vigorously rejected because it pictures the political environment as essentially irrational— a sphere of life dominated by negotiating and bargaining power. While it is true that budget decisions are influenced by "push, pull and pressure," this essay is based on an assumption that the political and administrative order is capable of responding to evidence and logic, provided that budgetmakers methodically introduce evidence and logic into their work.

10

Moreover, comparing budgeting work with the work of artisans suggests that the elements of good practice can be learned, and applied by persons of average endowment. In other words, one does not need higher mathematics or a college degree to master the secrets of the craft. The comparison also suggests that success in budgetmaking is related to artisan-like traits of methodical work, done to exacting standards. In budgeting, as in any craft, practice makes perfect!

Finally, true craftsmen pursue their work with few ulterior motives. Craftsmen take satisfaction from a job well done. This aspect of our craft ideal inspires budgetmakers to undertake improvements in budgetary practice, despite uncertain or disappointing rewards. This is to say that budgetmakers should improve their skills to perfect their competence, and, in the process, strengthen the technical basis of budgetmaking—both self-sufficient motivations for craftsmen.

As a craft, rather than an art, budgeting does not require virtuosic talent. This is an important distinction because "craftsmanship" implies that the intellectual and practical aspects of budgeting can be codified and the requisite knowledge and skill taught and learned. As appropriate action requires the light of reasoned thought, the title of this essay reflects my high regard for the intellectual foundations of budgetary craftsmanship.

A Note on the Essay Format

In closing this introduction to the revised and expanded edition of *Budgetary Thought for School Officials*, it is fitting that I comment on the rationale for its format. I drew my inspiration from the pedagogical approach, known in shorthand as the **SQ3R** Method. (Credited to Francis P. Robinson, 1946) Briefly described, this method embraces 1) synoptic **S**urveys, or gestalt, establishing relevant patterns, 2) active **Q**uestioning, and 3) application of procedures facilitating comprehension and remembrance: a) **R**eading, b) **R**ecitation and c) **R**eview. Consequently, this text emphasizes rationale, poses significant questions, and presents practical responses for the reader's consideration. Obviously, although recitation is recommended, its practice is a reader's option. Reviews of important points are presented at the end of each part. As the concepts of survey and questioning are essential instruments of critical thinking—the most important budgetary skill—the **SQ3R** Method, itself, should be applied by the reader to the study of this essay.

Also referencing proven pedagogy, I have invited readers to draft initial Benchmark and, then, closing Assessment Essays addressing the question, What is "good" budgeting. By so doing, readers can illuminate and document the intellectual impact of *Budgetary Thought for School Officials.*

Benchmark Essay

Clarify Your Thinking

Before engaging with the concepts and practices recommended herein, you are invited to take a moment to crystallize your current understanding of budgeting by drafting an essay addressing the question, What is "good" Budgeting? Completing this exercise will establish a personal benchmark for measuring the impact of your engagement with the concepts and practices recommended by *Budgetary Thought for School Officials*. Additionally, by organizing your thoughts, you will take the first step required by the above cited SQ3R method, that is, establishing a relevant initial mental framework (gestalt) for your study. Further, the exercise, itself, will probably generate more questions (SQ3R step 2), promoting interest in the concepts and practices to be presented by the text.

What Is "Good" Budgeting?

_____

_____

_____

_____

_____, etc.

If you feel that your Benchmark Essay did not respond well to the question, cheer up! Even experienced budgetmakers have trouble establishing acceptable criteria for judging what is "good" in a field marked by semantic and procedural confusion, and torn by basic conflicts of professional perspective and political interest. Regardless of the difficulty, however, educators, acting as budgetmakers, should make an attempt to think though the premises of their decisions to frame a set of criteria for the evaluation of their budget allocations.

At the close of *Budgetary Thought for School Officials*, you will be invited to address the same normative question. Posing this question again provides you with an opportunity to assess the impact of your engagement with its recommended concepts and practices.

1. On Budgets and Budgeting

What is "Good" Budgeting?

At this point the reader may fairly ask, how do I define "good" budgeting? My response follows. Its themes merit close attention.

Decades of experience demonstrate that the desire and pressure for public education is persistent and expansive. However, experience also indicates that measures to provide resources to satisfy this desire and pressure are resisted. Consequently, at any given time, educational authorities must ration limited resources. One may truly say that the employment of budgets and budgeting procedures is traceable to the incongruity of limited resources and limitless desire.

Identifying budgeting with rationing, is a fair and true definition, as far as it goes. However, it is also unquestionably true that the process of allocating scarce resources can be done well, poorly or even indifferently, depending on one's motivation and judgment criteria. Thus, we are challenged to address a normative question: "What is 'good' budgeting?" Reflecting my experience, this question produces a variety of responses. As indicated by the following observations, budgets, and budgeting, mean different things to different people, depending on vantage points and interests:

- To an economist, a "good" budget produces equivalent benefits at the margin of expenditure, that is, the last dollar spent on education, let us say, yields a benefit equal to that produced by the last dollar spent on other public purposes.

- To a student of politics, a "good" budget promotes civic morale by incorporating the interest of "interests" within the expenditure and revenue scheme.

- To a citizen/taxpayer, a "good" budget is "too low" for those programs favored by the citizen/taxpayer, and "too high" as an aggregate of all programs.

- To an elected official, such as a school board member, a "good" budget redeems the promises of the last campaign and consolidates support for the next.

- To a finance director, a "good" budget reflects accurate, balanced estimates, useful in financial planning and control.

In addition to variations in criteria which flow naturally from differences in perspective and/or interest, an adequate definition of "good" budgeting must come to terms with the semantic and procedural variety introduced into the field by advocates of four alternative approaches to traditional commodity-based Line-Item Budgeting (LIB). These are Performance Budgeting (PerB, Program Budgeting (ProB), Planning/Programming/Budgeting System (PPBS), and Zero-Base Budgeting (ZBB). In Part 2, *Budgetary Classification,* I have provided the reader with succinct definitions of these alternative approaches to the formatting and formulation of budgets.

Format Alternatives Provide a Clue

While these various alternatives to LIB invoke different techniques, all four are as one on this essential point:

> *Budget procedures and documentation should focus critical attention on 1) issues, problems and opportunities to be addressed, and 2) what is to be done (output) and achieved (outcome/impact).*

As solution-centered, results-oriented instruments, "good" budgets provide an efficacious *d*istribution of scarce resources, calculated to resolve issues, solve perceived problems and seize opportunities.

Further, as rationing is the essential cause and consequence of budgeting, the merit of budgets depends on:1) the relationship between allocated resources *(the less the better)* and stated purposes and *2)* the comparative worth of those purposes *(the more the better.* Thus, in addition to goal attainment, "good" budgets husband resources. Adding the values of *efficiency* and *economy* to *effectiveness* establishes an efficacy triad, useful for the objective appraisal of the merit of allocations.

"Good" Budgets Require a Diagnostic Foundation

Whether stated or not, every budget allocation challenges an undesired reality, proposing ways and means of elimination or amelioration. Consequently, the first step in school budget formulation should be an exploration of perplexities, that is, demonstrated deficiencies in student knowledge and/or skill to be addressed by programmatic solutions. Most assuredly, thinking about desired results implies that there are perplexities to challenge, ameliorate, and, perhaps, banish. If done proficiently, this recommended diagnostic step will not only provide a rationale for allocating scarce resources to attain desired results, but also serves to help identify the critical, or controlling, variables that must be programmatically addressed to secure goal attainment. Consequently, "good" budgets are founded on sufficient understanding of the perplexities to be programmatically addressed. This diagnostic step is also crucial for budget implementation as, logically, program effectiveness cannot be measured unless desired results are related to specified conditions. *The importance of the diagnostic step cannot be overstated.*

It has been often noted that people working in institutional settings tend to confound processes with purposes. Educators, acting in their budgetmaking capacity, are no less addicted to confounding processes with purposes, and budget accordingly. This pervasive mental habit produces inefficacious budgets. Such budgets may look solid, but the confounding of means and ends inevitably leads to misallocation. For example, "teaching" costs are commonly classified as "instruction" in school budgets. Of course, the process of instruction must be funded, but, logically, paying teachers to teach is funding a secondary objective. The primary objective of education is student achievement, that is, desired changes in student mental capabilities. Consequently, "good" school budgets are focused by the diagnosis of continuing and emergent student learning issues, problems and opportunities. Unless they explicitly devote resources to resolving issues, solving problems, and seizing opportunities, presented as perplexities, school budget documents are superficial "mission" statements. They assert what is intended, but not why!

Formats Reflect and Shape Budgetary Thought

Shifting the expression of budgetary thinking from "teaching" to "learning" is more than terminological slight-of-hand. Budget formats and formulation procedures that explicitly relate allocations to student performance may be confidently expected to stimulate thinking about critical learning variables, such as, learning readiness, curriculum sequence, and, especially, time-on-task, and its dynamic classroom adjustment based on demonstrations of achievement, or lack thereof.

An exercise demonstrating the influence of formats on budgetary thinking is presented in Part 2, *Budgetary Classification.* In addition to considering commodities to be bought, a solution-centered, results-oriented budget might state that "x" dollars are to be allocated to attain the promotion of "y" 4th graders to the 5th grade, with an estimated failure rate of "z" percent. Or, better yet, "x" dollars are allocated to attain the goal of "y" percent of 4th grade students reading at grade level, as attested by student achievement. This form of classifying the purpose of allocations encourages budgetmakers to apply objective evaluation criteria, such as, 1) performance ratios, (relating teacher and student time-on-task to achievement objectives), 2) investment returns (relating ascribed benefits to program costs), and 3) correlations (relating critical learning variables to achievement).

Budgets as Communication: Literary Criteria

One final point: Because an adopted budget represents an understanding between appropriation authorities and interested and affected parties on what is to be done, bought or sought, the style and content of the document should meet literary, rather than public relations standards. An informative content, clarity and brevity are the prized virtues. Published budgets should be compact and readable, the acid test being the ability of interested and affected parties to gain an unaided grasp of the program and performance implications of expenditures and revenues. Budget narratives should integrate and explain all numerical displays. Of course, this means that a great deal of thought must go into the layout of budget pages. Pages should be printed on both sides. Summaries need to be carefully organized, as they control the number of program titles to be shown, hence the number of pages required.

The literary quality of budget documents depends on topic selection and emphasis. The rules are: 1) choose a level of abstraction which does justice to the issues, problems and opportunities addressed by each program, and 2) avoid extensive detail (there is no space to waste) and generalities.

In addition to accuracy in all computations and estimates, every budget document should reflect the underlying thought. See Part 6, *Formulation,* for recommendations to that effect. Accordingly, the format and content of published budgets, should summarize detailed budget formulation documentation, This strain toward textual correspondence also tends to ensure that the literary ideals of "good" budgeting are widely diffused among those participating in the process.

Key Thoughts in Review

As a form of rationing, budgeting is defined as a principled craft to be learned and practiced, requiring objective evidence and logic applied to the task of allocation.

Addressing diagnosed perplexities, defined as issues, problems and opportunities, "good" budgets fund solutions, that is, expected student achievements and attainments.

The literary quality of budget documents depends on topic selection and emphasis.

---

2. Budgetary Classification

What's in a Name?

The human mind never ceases to classify the manifold facts of life. It is this tendency to classify which provides the foundation of human knowledge, the basis for individual understanding, and the vehicle for social communication. In the preface to his classic, *Government Budgeting* (1956), Jesse Burkhead pointed out the budgetary significance of classification with this comment: " ... the way in which revenue and expenditure are grouped for decision-making is the most important aspect of budgeting."

To assess the import of Professor Burkhead's observation, I have provided an exercise in classification on the next page. In this exercise, you are to imagine that you are an educational policymaker. It's budget adoption time. In a workshop session covering secondary school programs, you are reviewing a recently submitted proposed annual budget for a Technical High School.

Budget Presented in a Commodity Format

The proposed budget, summarized as Exhibit 2.1, *A Technical High School Budget,* is classified by commodities, thus, it is an example of a Line-Item Budget (LIB). Essentially line-item budgets are accounting statements. The numbers may be accompanied by narratives which explain changes in organization, salary costs, school supplies, etc.

EXHIBIT 2.1 A Technical High School Budget (Line-Item)

This Year	Classification	Budget	+/-
4,725,000	Personal Services	4,800,000	+75,000
455,000	Non-Personal Expense	480,000	+25,000
220,000	Contractual Services	240,000	+20,000
600,000	Outlay	480,000	- 120,000
6,000,000	Total	6,000,000	

This type of budget format does not help readers grasp the programmatic, much less the performance implications of proposed expenditures. Review the expenditure display. Remember that you are a policymaker attending a budget workshop with your colleagues and accountable administrators. As questions come to mind, jot them down in the space provided.

Your Questions

_____

_____

_____, etc.

The Budget Reclassified

Now, review Exhibit 2.2, *A Technical High School Budget.* The same expenditures are classified differently.

EXHIBIT 2.2 A Technical High School Budget (Performance)

This Year	Classification	Budget	+/-
2,310,000	Academic Achievement	2,410,000	+100,000
3,690,000	Vocational Achievement	3,590,000	- 100,000
6,000,000	Total	6,000,000	

This Year	Performance Data	Budget	+/-
95%	% Above Mathematics Norm	98%	+3%
93%	% Above Reading Norm	95%	+2%
92%	Attendance Ratio	95%	+3%
90%	Graduation Ratio	95%	+5%

Unit Measure

1,500	Number of Students	1,500	
$4,000	Unit Cost	4,000	

The expenditures are identified by concepts that point up what is to be done, or sought, rather than what is to be bought. Note that the expenditure display is accompanied by a performance data array. It is this combination of "activity" titles and associated expected results which makes a "performance" budget. Jot down your questions about this reclassified budget in the space provided.

Your Questions

_____
_____
_____,etc.

Now, compare the two question lists. Reflecting my experience with this exercise, the lists of questions will vary significantly, providing a lesson in the power of formats to influence thinking, and, thus, decisions.

Format Importance Emphasized

There is little question that a "commodity" format invites (almost compels) thinking and discussion about things to be bought, rather than directing attention to perplexities, policies and procedures. Furthermore, a display of commodities often tempts reviewing officials to alter the expenditure pattern in ways which are unrelated to policy issues and/or service levels. All too often, such changes (usually reductions) are not accompanied by explanations or expressions of intent. In contrast, the reclassified budget, Exhibit 2.2, invites discussion about the relationship of expenditures to performance indicators and goals. They draw attention to such issues as the opportunity costs of shifting resources (and time-on-task) from one objective to another, and the marginal productivity of investments in higher student attainment, for example, fewer "drop-outs" and more graduates. On principle, analytically acute interpretive narratives should accompany arrays associating programmatic expenditures with performance data.

***The point to remember: Formats are important!
People tend to think about what comes before them.***

As previously indicated, over the years, budgetmakers have developed five basic classification schemes:

- Line-Item Budgeting (LIB)
- Performance Budgeting (PerB)
- Program Budgeting (ProB)
- Planning/Programming/Budgeting System (PPBS)
- Zero-Base Budgeting (ZBB)

Each format is distinguished by supporting procedures and analytical techniques. At this point, review the matrix, Exhibit 2.3, *Budget Formats*. It supplements salient characteristics of each format with definitions of its rationale.

EXHIBIT 2.3 Budget Formats

	CHARACTERISTICS	THE QUESTION	ORIENTATION	CRITERION
LIB	- Expenditures & revenues related to commodities	What is to be bought?	Control	Economy
PerB	- Expenditures & revenues related to workloads - Cost center arrays - Performance data arrays	What is to be done?	Management	Efficiency
ProB	- Expenditures & revenues related to goals - Trans-organizational cost centers.	What is to be achieved?	Planning	Effectiveness
PPBS	- Expenditures & revenues related to goals & benefits - Trans-organizational cost centers - Analysis of alternatives - Multi-year projections	What is to be achieved?	Planning	Effectiveness
ZBB	- Expenditures & revenues. related to workloads - Cost center arrays - Limited historical data - Ranking of alternative proposals	What is to be done?	Management	Efficiency

Experienced budgetmakers (and political leaders) do not regard formats with neutrality. In pure form, each format is thought to produce (or reflect) a unique ethos, or policy bearing. In this regard, the practice of LIB is deemed to flourish in environments dominated by control and economic values. PerB and ZBB, on the other hand, are thought to express official interest in management and efficiency values. Officials interested in planning and goal attainment are thought to favor ProB and PPBS procedures. The distinction between "What is to be done?" and "What is to be achieved?" is subtle, but fundamental. Ask yourself this question: Would a budget justified by student achievement and attainment be the same as one justified by teaching loads expressed as pupil/teacher ratios.

An example of budgetary formatting and classification may be found in Appendix A, *An Annotated Model Published Budget.* Applied to allocations for a technical high school, it displays an annotated version of a budget presentation suitable for publication and review by policymakers, parents and citizens. It expands on the previous exhibits regarding allocations for a technical high school. Before reviewing and evaluating Appendix A, take a moment to consult your thinking about the public documentation of a public school budget. Use the space provided below to jot down your documentation criteria:

_____
_____
_____
_____
_____,etc.

Now, compare your thoughts with the concepts outlined by the commentary concerning literary criteria at the close of Part 1. Next, evaluate the solution-centered, results-oriented budget displayed in Appendix A, comparing its form and content with your specifications, Also, compare your criteria with the form and content of familiar published education budgets. These comparisons should prove illuminating. This exercise has achieved it purpose if it has heightened your awareness of the impact of format and classification on budgetary thought and action.

Before turning to considerations of administrative and accounting foundations, two points about budget classification deserve emphasis:

- Budget documentation is the result of topic selection and emphasis, wherein the author(s) takes on moral responsibility (this metaphysical function is not often unrecognized) for defining reality for other people.

- Topics, supporting narratives and data arrays should faithfully mirror the underlying analytical thinking.

The first point alerts budgetmakers at all levels, particularly those who compose manuscripts for published budget documents, to their responsibility, and their opportunity. The second point enjoins budgetmakers to search for just the right level of factual detail, and interpretation, which can assist policymakers to make wise allocations of scarce resources—the master problem of budgeting. Budget documents incorporating narrative displays have become fairly common. By and large, however, budgets tend to be accounting statements, filled with lines of figures, intelligible only to those who prepare them.

> *Certainly, any serious attempt to practice solution-centered, results-oriented budgeting requires appropriate attention to the level and type of documentation.*

Every program has its unique presentation requirements, which may change from year to year. In this connection, the standardization of cost centers, and their stability over the years for the sake of annual comparisons is certainly important, but should not be an overriding consideration. It is much more important to be able to focus policymaking attention on the significant issues, problems and opportunities of each program. In some years, this may mean a more extensive breakdown of program titles, or fewer, depending on the level of aggregation needed to deepen consideration of the perplexities addressed. An adequate scheme of cost centers must be so organized that they can be related to measures of output, outcome and impact, assisting budgetmakers in assessing the intrinsic and relative merit of allocations. Most assuredly, the classification scheme must include identifiers for the most important of educational resources: *teacher and student time-on-task*. Often, a scheme of cost centers must cross organizational lines, and require the cooperation of several program managers, to aggregate the costs of significant programmatic thrusts. For example, in addition to classroom teachers, elementary school programs require subject matter specialists in art, music, mathematics, foreign languages, etc.; who are usually funded by disparate cost centers. Accurate costing of programs in complex organizations, such as many contemporary public schools, requires cross-classified cost centers, that is, cost center arrays which display the same total cost distributed to different activities and/or purposes. (For example, the time of subject matter specialists distributed to classroom data arrays of teacher and student time-0n-task.) Providing multi-dimensional contexts, rather than the customary mono-dimensional presentations, cross-classified budgets expand the range of budgetary thought and action.

Key Thoughts in Review

Formats are important because the organization and presentation of information affects thinking and decisions. By broadening and deepening insight, cross-classified budgets are particularly valuable. Addressing perplexities and expected results, flexible formats are deemed more desirable than standardized classification schemes.

Despite acknowledged problems, an adequate scheme of cost centers is essential. Even if there is a tendency to overstate the influence of formats on decision-making, people do tend to think about what comes before them. The classification of expenditures and revenues shapes thought and discussion, and, thus, the action agenda.

Solution-centered, results-oriented budgeting requires a flexible and elaborate scheme of cost centers. Often, subsidiary ledgers are needed to split or allocate costs, or to distribute previously recorded expenditures. Be warned, many accountants resist the elaboration of accounts required by performance and program budgets because it creates serious coding, control and reconciliation problems.

3. Administrative and Accounting Foundations

... explores the prerequisites of suggested decision-making machinery, including solution-centered, results-oriented budgeting.

For decades, in the interest of effectiveness, efficiency and economy (the efficacy triad), educational authorities in the United States have been consolidating public school districts. This movement has been tracked over the years by the U.S. Census of Governments, which records that the number of public school districts dropped from 108,579 in 1942 to 38,266 in 2012. This significant reduction is evidence that educational authorities respond to efficacy considerations, especially the positive effects of scale on curriculum offerings. However, increasing the scale of operations also encourages, permits, even compels, the development of bureaucratic practices and expressions of "bureaupathic" behavior. Having a noble purpose does not exempt institutions from the dysfunctions associated with organizational scale and complexity. For many who find their hearth and altar in formal organizations, organizational means readily become personal ends.

> *Consequently, it is very important that educational authorities establish and actively use decision-making machinery that ensures that 1) the time and effort of students is valued more highly than that of school employees, and 2) information about student achievements and attainments, or lack thereof, drive the budget process.*

At minimum, the suggested decision-making machinery supports. a solution-centered, results-oriented approach to budget formulation and implementation that justifies proposed investments by 1) identifying the perplexities (issues, problems and opportunities) to be addressed, 2) the proposed solutions, and 3) the specific results to be attained, in addition to the services and commodities to be acquired through expenditures.

This suggested budgetary approach deserves support by a) decision-related research, principally mathematical modeling, assessing the impact of selected variables thought likely to influence student performance, and b) management accounting. By considering and applying information produced by reliance on the suggested decision-making machinery, educational authorities can better focus scarce resources, enhancing the impact of variables proven most effective.

> **Decision-Related Research.** Regarding mathematical modeling, few, if any, school authorities are reported relying on systematic correlation studies to illuminate the relative effects of variables thought to influence student performance. Models define an ordered set of assumptions about causes, effects and objectives. By using models to specify relationships between variables thought to "make a difference" in performance, educators can enhance their ability to attain, and sustain, a desired level of educational effectiveness. (Likely examples of significant variables are *actual measurements* of time-on-task, verbal facility of teachers, teacher feedback to students on their performance, and parental interest) Computers have put mathematical modeling within easy reach of educational authorities, done in-house or commercially. In-house resources should include math teachers and students. For a sample correlation, see Appendix C, *An Indicative Illustration of Modeling Procedures.*

> **Management Accounting**. Typically, public education accounting concentrates on recording and controlling expenditures and logging revenues. Supplementing this basic accounting arrangement with management-style accounting can provide education authorities with a

flexible system of accounts for recording and reporting effort, measured by costs and/or work time. This capability facilitates the formulation and adoption of solution-centered, results-oriented budgets relating costs and work plans to programs and activities. Significantly, management accounting can facilitate the planning and tracking of teacher and student time-on-task related to subject matter and results. Giving actual measurements of student time-on-task a prominent role in the budgetary thought of educators would certainly place school budgets on a very strong foundation. An example of a forth grade performance budget work plan is displayed by Exhibit 6.3, *A Sample Work Plan.*

Solution-Centered, Results-Oriented Budgets. Public education budgets typically aggregate and display expenditure by abstract categories, such as instruction, plant maintenance, etc., and associated expenditure requirements, such as salaries, textbooks, paint etc. Although listing items of procurement is necessary for calculating expenditure estimates, this approach to budgeting (Line-Item Budgeting) does not automatically draw attention to the relationship of resources to salient indicators of educational efficacy. In contrast, performance and program budget formats foster and support solution-centered, results-oriented budgetary thinking. Consequent commentary will explore the cognitive and documentary implications of a suggested solution-centered, results-oriented budgetary approach.

Specifically, the administrative and accounting determinants of successful implementation of solution-centered, results-oriented budgets are 1) effective articulation and use of performance data; 2) an elaborate, flexible classification and coding scheme; 3) accounting procedures which facilitate the aggregation of non-monetary performance data, formally correlated with measures of effort and monetary data; and 4) continuous management utilization of four interrelated instruments of budget implementation. These instruments embrace a) work plans, b) allotments, c) dynamic monitoring via periodic formal performance reviews and d) timely corrective action to forestall failure to achieve objectives.   Effective budgeting (attainment of performance objectives) is best assured by using an institutional framework integrating these determinants, with accounting procedures providing the glue. Mutually reinforcing, the absence or limp implementation of any of these determinants reduces the effectiveness of the others.

Installing the mechanics of a data-driven approach, as suggested, has significant managerial implications. Mutually supporting management accounting and budgeting procedures endow accountable educators with the ability to establish a flexible scheme of identifiers, useful for aggregating selected data at various points and levels of concern. A flexible classification capability provides expanded opportunities to encourage, register and validate the active participation of staff, students, parents and other interested parties in the conduct of a data-driven educational enterprise. In particular, teachers can be provided opportunities to register their programmatic concerns and plans in the classification system, ensuring that "classroom reality," that complex of transactions between teachers and students, is effectively represented in the matrix of critical variables guiding the implementation of a data-driven approach.

The illuminating value of data-based approach to education practice was demonstrated by James S. Coleman, et al., when, in 1966, they conducted a large scale Congressionally-mandated correlation study of variables conventionally thought to contribute to the educational effectiveness of the public schools. The study report, *Equality of Educational Opportunity*, cast doubt on the educational effectiveness of all but one of the selected school-based "causal" variables. Surprisingly, the school-based variables showing no significant correlation with student performance included such icons of public school practice as class size, teacher experience, and except in the segregated situation of the schools of the American South, per pupil expenditure. Most important, and most controversial, the researchers concluded that social characteristics of the students, and student/family-centered variables, rather than school practices, were predictors of student performance. In other words, what happens in school is less responsible for differences in student performance than the impact of characteristics the student carries into the school.

Additionally, at the time of this writing, geneticists probing DNA impacts on behavior report correlations between genetic endowments and academic achievement and attainment. Expanding knowledge of genetic predispositions in human life and behavior is already affecting decisions, public and private. One may expect that research into the role of DNA in human life and development will also affect educational theory and practice in the future.

With reference to the one statistically significant in-school causal variable, the Colman study found that the *verbal facility score* of teachers was the *only* school-based variable significantly related to student performance, *ceteris paribus*. In terms of budgetary thinking, it is noteworthy that this salient finding about the influence of verbal facility has had no apparent impact on teacher recruitment and retention practices. Teachers with high verbal facility reportedly do not stay in teaching for long. If true, this has implications for recruitment and compensation because their leaving weakens the teaching cohort with respect to this key impact variable. Paradoxically, across the United States, public school systems generally base teacher compensation on academic attainment and time-in-service, two variables found wanting by the Coleman study.

Reports concerning the contemporary educational situation across America's public schools strongly suggest that educational authorities and researchers have not been notably successful in identifying and eliminating ineffective in-school practices in favor of those that promise to overcome and/or neutralize the sociological determinants of student performance. Adding to the stress, in the years since 1966, critical attention shifted from concern with the impact of resource disparities on student performance (horizontal equity) to attempts to attain equal outcomes, that is, students achieving prescribed levels of performance (vertical equity). This shift in attention resulted in the adoption of the "no child left behind" legislation in 2001, and other similar student achievement-based efforts since.

Controversial then, and controversial now, the Coleman Report findings have disquieting implications because they subvert the common notion that educational practice matters. Indeed, these findings provide no support for school-centered initiatives currently underway, such as "common core," which affirm the intrenched belief that organized pedagogy trumps sociology! Even more unsettling for many Americans, the conclusions of the Coleman Report provide support for public investments in socio-economic engineering initiatives rather than direct investments in school programming. At this point, fifty plus years after the publication of the Coleman Report, America's primary and secondary schools are engaged in a grand experiment that is testing the power of organized pedagogy to overcome socio-economic influences hampering the educational progress of many students.

In general, educational authorities are responding to the pressure for increased student cognitive performance with traditional measures, including teaching to tests, reducing class size, and tracking students for remediation and tutoring. Additional attempts to improve educational effectiveness, measured by cognitive competence, include the arbitrary imposition of higher academic standards, school choice vouchers, charter schools and tuition tax credit schemes.

Only recently have educational authorities started exploiting the revolutionary potential of information technology to provide knowledge transfer and skill development, independent of traditional education methodology and location. Thus far, this movement is having marginal effects on the organization and procedures of institutions of higher learning and little discernible effects on primary and secondary schools, the locus of truly critical problems. Whatever their merits, however, the favored institutional and financial solutions represent indirect approaches to changing pedagogic processes, where, in plain language, "the rubber meets the road!"

As stated in my introductory note, it would seem preferable, and less expensive and disruptive, to try. approaches which explicitly aim to provide educational leaders, institution by institution, with decision-making machinery and implementation instruments that can help them focus scarce resources on variables proven most likely to enhance student performance.

Typically, educational institutions are conservatively governed and managed. Clearly, the inertia of enormous investments in school plant and teaching methodologies, and, most notably, influential entrenched interests, limit the discretion of educational authorities. To be sure, when the proofs of the past coincide with the conditions of the present, traditions provide a way, and a life. But when tradition degrades into mere precedent, it is useful only to rearguards disputing the ground before the advance of new techniques, or superseding ideas. The educational use of computers provides a critical case in point. When computers first emerged, and for decades after, educational authorities responded in traditional terms by adding "computer literacy" to the curriculum. Most assuredly, educators recognized the potential of computers for information transfer, skill development and diagnostics, but shrank with fear and dread from the institutional implications of technology which empowers students, rather than the traditional system.

Consequently, despite the expansion in the educational usage of computers, countless millions of students continue to find that education means schoolhouses and classrooms, students grouped by age or interest, teacher's telling and questioning, upraised hands and chalkboard demonstrations. As pointed out previously, on the evidence, traditional practice produces uneven results. Large numbers of students perform indifferently while in school. Numerous students fail to finish secondary school. Significant numbers graduating from high school are found poorly prepared for college. Aside from application of computer-facilitated pedagogy, educational authorities possess no practical remedy for these critical concerns. Indeed, those currently interested in enhancing educational effectiveness tend to favor institutional and financial solutions cited above.

This essay advances the thesis that, in addition to these approaches, educators need a methodology to

find and eliminate relatively ineffective pedagogic processes in favor of those proving effective.

Ironically, educators have long enjoyed access to research on educational effectiveness. However, excepting the path-finding 1966 study report, *Equality of Educational Opportunity, 1966,* educational research embraces relatively small samples and the narrow research concerns of academia. Consequently, this research tends to lack explicit decision, or operational foci, such as badly-needed cost/effective studies. Most critically, the research literature abounds with contradictory, inconsistent observations and conclusions, discouraging educators who would like to apply research results to educational programming and budgeting. The inadequacy of research-based guidance concerning educational effectiveness also helps to account for the inertia of educational authorities in confronting the challenge to traditional practice.

Based on abundant reports regarding the current state of the public schools and the struggle to meet the goal of steadily improving student performance, it is evident that public school authorities could use improved decision-making machinery and implementation instruments that can help them focus scarce resources on program variables proven most likely to enhance student performance. Given the likely persistence of traditional practice, despite the spotty record of effectiveness, what can be done to provide accountable educators with access to valid, objective, site-specific, decision-related information about the relative efficacy of key factors affecting learning outcomes?

To recapitulate, this essay advances the proposition that accountable educators can significantly improve student performance, institution-by-institution, by installing decision-making machinery and implementation instruments that integrate 1) decision-related research, principally mathematical modeling, 2) management accounting, and 3) results-oriented budgeting procedures. Once available, educators should be encouraged to use this integrated system of procedures to assess the impact of selected variables influencing pupil performance. With assessments in hand, educators can use the information produced by this system to allocate scarce resources to enhance the impact of variables proven most effective.

In concluding this commentary on decision-making machinery, the suggested approach affirms the idea that schools have "production functions," meaning that variations in in-school educational practice have significant effects on educational results, variously measured. This proposal assumes that school officials will pursue rational policy and management practices, that is, base decisions on end-means relationships, when these are identified and validated. This approach also encourages educational authorities to factor out-of-school variables into the decision-making machinery and implementation instruments. Consequently, in addition to identifying relative efficacy of in-school programmatic variables, this approach can provide very valuable information about socio-economic factors related to student performance, information which can inspire lawmakers to address the socio-economic issues raised by the Coleman Report.

Key Thoughts in Review

Educational authorities should establish and actively use decision-making machinery that ensures that 1) the time and effort of students is valued more highly than that of their employees, and 2) information about student achievements and attainments, or lack thereof, drives the budget process.

The recommended data-driven approach requires 1) decision-related research, (principally, correlation studies assessing the impact of selected variables thought likely to influence student performance), 2) management accounting and 3) solution-centered, results-oriented budgeting.

Relying on correlations, the well-known study, *Equality of Educational Opportunity,* by James S. Colman, et al., cast doubt on the educational effectiveness of all but one of the selected school-based "causal" variables, the verbal facility of teachers.

4. Budgetmaker's Toolbox

... outlines subjective and objective tools and techniques applied to evaluate and justify fund allocations.

As previously noted, when educators turn their attention to budgeting, they are thinking in terms of the fundamental process, that is, rationing scarce resources. As this task requires judgment, it is obvious that they apply appraisal criteria. Thus, the choice of appraisal criteria is critically important, and determinative.

As also noted in the discussion of craft ideals, budgetmakers should strive to give their work a solid technical foundation, and an ideal development. In craft work, planning and performance are an integrated process. Budgetmakers aspiring to the craft ideal appreciate this axiom, and seek to establish an interplay between theory and practice. As an ideal, we have established budgetmaking as a thought process about the worth of things, in addition to considerations about the price of things. In order to make judgments worthy of this ideal, budgetmakers must assess (1) the relationship of resources to purposes, and, (2) the relative worth of those purposes as objects of investment. To pursue these key tasks with proficiency, budget makers can apply an ensemble of considerations, a craftsman's box of tools and techniques, as it were. Identified as pragmatic or formal, Exhibit 4.1, *Allocation Criteria*, lists a set of considerations applied by budgetmakers to evaluate and justify their allocation decisions.

Before proceeding, I should make it clear that I am assuming that budgets have "production functions," that is, I believe that alternatives in educational investment do have performance consequences. (This is an important distinction because, as the reader will recall, the evidence presented by the Coleman Report cast doubt on the production function of the public schools.). Consequently, for my purpose here, the production function of an institution's budget is an integral aspect of the production function of the institution itself.

As the key thrust of budgetary thinking, I advanced the idea that budgetmakers should seek to identify efficacious relationships between resources applied (the less the better) and desired results, (the more the better). In this endeavor, educational officials will find that the application of "formal" allocation criteria is not only helpful, but essential. The repertoire of formal criteria noted in Exhibit 4.1, *Allocations Criteria*, in particular, performance ratios, are useful because they relate investments in cost and effort to results. Applying formal considerations enable budgetmakers to understand and specify the "production function" of budgets. Consequently, one might safely say, that the production function of an educational budget (and by inference, the executing institution) can be best attained by satisfying formal, that is, objective, criteria.

Mathematically, the "production function" of a budget can be described by the equation, $y = f(x)$,.where "x" represents a budget allocation, "y" equals the benefit (monetized, if possible; if not, specified in numerical or physical terms), and "*f*" symbolizes the production technique, such as, verbal or chalkboard instruction, drill and practice, programmed learning procedures, homework, etc. Generally, we assume that "y" (the output) depends on "x" (the input), and that the output should increase or decrease as the input increases or decreases. We also know that investments are subject to the so-called law of "diminishing returns," which warns us that, after a certain point, more input may produce increased output, but at a declining rate. Accordingly, different levels of resource deployment for a given program produce different amounts of benefit. (The varying utilities of program investments are graphically described by a "lazy 'S' curve" relating investments to benefits.) Hence, budgetmakers are advised to think about the impact of investments in curvilinear, rather than linear terms.

The practical advantages of using mathematical procedures in the budget appraisal process are secondary to their conceptual utility. Their use provokes the right questions. Although data deficiencies limit the practical application of mathematics to relationships between budget allocations and their effects, their conceptual impact encourages budget officers to focus on varying relationships between input and output variables. Equations belong in every budgetmaker's toolbox.

At this point consult Exhibit 4.1, *Allocation Criteria*. It identifies characteristic considerations applied by budgetmakers to justify judgments about the merit of proposals. The reader will note that these considerations are classified as pragmatic or formal—depending on whether they are applied expediently, or on principle.

EXHIBIT 4.1 Allocation Criteria

PRAGMATIC	FORMAL

INERTIA
    Organizational and programmatic continuities.
 	
COMPLEMENTARITIES
    Services supporting other services.
 	
DISEQUILIBRIA
    Correcting imbalances; redressing grievances;. restoring conditions.
	SERVICE STANDARDS
	    Market. Equity
	    Equal Allocation of Resources
	    Equal Results
	
	PERFORMANCE RATIOS
	Efficiency
	    Cost/Results
	    Results/Cost
	    Work Time/Results
	    Results/Work Time
	Effectiveness
	    Goal Attainment Percentage
	Programmatic
	    Unique Ratios
	
	MODELING
	    Correlation
	
	INVESTMENT RETURNS
	    Investment Yield
	    Marginal Productivity
	
	WEIGHTING AND SCORING
	    Ordinal Ranking
	    Multi-dimensional Scoring

In consulting Exhibit 4.1, *Allocation Criteria*, the reader will note that it classifies three justifications as "pragmatic." Significantly, throughout the world, budgetmakers find pragmatic considerations persuasive in justifying budget allocations. Budgetmakers can be said to be behaving "pragmatically" when they respond existentially, that is, they accept, willing or not, existing situations.

In contrast, the "formal" considerations listed in Exhibit 4.1 are concepts of evaluation and justification that are to be applied "on-principle," regardless of the situation. According to our normative ideal of "good" budgeting, budgetmakers should always strive to justify allocations by reference to formal, rather than pragmatic criteria. (Of course, their mere calculation and appearance in budget documentation provides no guarantee that their application will influence allocation decisions.)

The list of formal considerations includes service standards, performance ratios, modeling, investment criteria and weighting and scoring procedures. These considerations and the conditions of their applications will be explored shortly. Each of these formal considerations, when proficiently applied, can illuminate, and objectify, the relationship of proposed allocations to educational issues, problems and opportunities. By applying these analytical tools and techniques, educators can clarify the *intrinsic* and *relative* merit of expenditures, the essential task in the efficacious rationing of resources.

Pragmatic Allocation Criteria

The decision-influencing power of inertia, complementarities and disequilibria is undeniable. Applying one or more of these terms to any given budget allocation endows it with a certain subjective form of merit in the eyes of ever-pragmatic officials. Each is briefly discussed, as follows:

Inertia. Drawn from the language of physics, "inertia" provides an apt description of the universal practice of re-appropriation, often with only cursory review of programmatic rationale. This phenomenon results in the relative stability of budget allocations over time, as budgetmakers tend to support established programs and services. And, why not? The inertial factor reflects the very essence of social life, fostered and maintained by our institutions.

This phenomenon also accounts for the low appeal of budgeting approaches which raise serious questions about existing service policies, "zero-base" budgeting, for example. After all, our institutions facilitate and stabilize society, serving perceived private wants and public needs. To do so requires a significant degree of organizational and service continuity. Consequently, a very high proportion of proposed school budgets fund existing programmatic and service units for another year of operation. And of this amount, a very high proportion is devoted to funding staff costs. For many educators, these two purposes provide sufficient evidence of merit, as they may be loath to do anything, but carp, about costs. The reality of "inertia" is succinctly summed up by program managers when they label their spending proposals "inescapable recurrent expenditure." The ready annual funding of the budget "base", albeit amended, testifies to the inertial power of established institutions. As a well-known case in point, President James Carter, in submitting the first budget of his presidency, lamented that he found 76 percent of the total to be relatively "uncontrollable."

This tendency to accept the "base" of proposed budgets is typically accompanied by a lively interest in incremental changes (usually additions). Of course, proposed increments to any given base budget, once adopted, fade into the base presented in the next budget cycle. The result is appropriately called "expenditure creep," a relentless upward trend in budget totals, over time. The best way to combat the influence of inertia is to identify possibilities for *goal displacement and means substitution* in established programs and services. Further comment on this important focus of budgetary craftsmanship is provided in the discussion of marginal productivity below.

Complementarities. Allocations which support other allocations are also given due weight. An educational district of any size will include many programmatic units dependent on services from central process units whose specialists service all units. Curriculum, finance, personnel, legal, engineering and maintenance functions are typically established as central process agencies. Adding or expanding programmatic services indirectly puts pressure on intra-institutional supporting services. Applied to budgeting, the concept of complementarity attests to the web-like nature of institutional activities. As a rule, appropriation authorities tend to support expenditure linked to other approved expenditures, or to decisions previously made, e.g., operating and maintenance expenditures related to opening a new school. Requirements for documentation of complementarities are noted in Part 6. See Exhibit 6.1, Statement 3, *Collaborators and Affected Parties*, for documentation requirements concerning complementarities. Budgetmakers have a special responsibility to closely review relationships between budget allocations, especially those supporting the service delivery capabilities of centralized process agencies serving programmatic units.

Disequilibria. In democracies, the leaders of public institutions are expected to respond to perceived problems of society. This response can be programmatic, financial or regulatory. Regardless of its form, assistance is provided to help correct perceived inequities and imbalances affecting various interests in the social and economic environment. As a case in point, from the beginning, with the adoption of compulsory educations laws, the public schools were visualized as vehicles to attain specific socio-economic aims. Evidence of constant pressure to address problems agitating the citizenry is seen in an ever-present flow of proposals to "do something" about some form or other of citizen behavior deemed harmful by somebody or other. In this regard, one thinks of driver education, bi-lingual education, all-day kindergarten and textbook purchasing practices as concessions to social and political demands. Once established, these programs tend to be regarded as "sacred cows," that is, requiring "inescapable, recurrent support." Many proposals to solve social problems through public educational programs prove impractical, but enough with budgetary implications do get adopted to justify identifying "disequilibria" as a significant pragmatic criterion.

Formal Allocation Criteria

Objective assessment of the intrinsic and relative merit of allocations is a formidable task, requiring the application of formal allocation criteria. Ideally, all concerned (elected officials, administrators and citizens) should strive to enlarge the role of formal allocation criteria in budgetary decisions.

Intrinsic Merit. Proposed allocations may be said to have *intrinsic* merit if their estimated programmatic affects and effects satisfy objective criteria, principally, the desired tendencies of the performance ratios listed in Exhibit 4.1.

Relative Merit. Proposed allocations may be said to have *relative* merit if their estimated programmatic affects and effects are deemed more valuable, on objective grounds, than those attributed to potential competitive allocations. Obviously, selecting proposed allocations to be made subject to such comparisons is a key decision, which should, if possible, reflect the application of objective criteria. Selection criteria might include, for example, all new programs, and all allocations involving requests for a) added staffing, b) expenditure increases and decreases exceeding a set amount or percent, or c) "overtime" payroll payments. Once grouping have been assembled, investment returns and weighting and scoring criteria can help to assess the relative merit of proposed allocations.

To help assess the merit of proposed allocations, Exhibit 4.1 lists five methods of formal evaluation, that is, concepts applied on principle. It should be noted that, in contrast to the relatively effortless application of pragmatic criteria, the employment of mathematics-based formal allocation criteria requires significant mental effort, mathematical savvy and pertinent performance data. In best practice, during the budget formulation and documentation phase, educational authorities should require that the accountable administrative and program officials apply formal evaluation criteria, appropriately drawn from the available repertoire.

The recommended guidelines for budget formulation and documentation advanced in Part 6, *Formulation and Documentation,* and Part 7, *Adoption*, assume that the information so assembled will enable educational authorities, at adoption time, to assess the intrinsic and relative merit of proposed allocations. Further, the diagnostic and analytical process used in budget formulation should be disclosed in pertinent public budget documentation. These practices represent the first line of effort for educational authorities interested in adopting allocations that have been subjected to objective tests of merit. The secondary line of effort requires sharp questioning of accountable administrative and program officials, referencing and applying the repertoire of formal allocation criteria. Most assuredly, when appropriation authorities show interest in applying formal allocation criteria, subordinate officials will also.

Service Standards.

Throughout the United States, service standards are an ever present influence on the budgetary thought of public school officials, especially mandates imposed by law and regulation. Most assuredly, standards imposed by law and pursuant regulations, and those associated with grants-in-aid, effectively reduce budgetary discretion. Obviously, officials must strive to comply with mandated standards.

A caution is in order, however, because even when proposed allocations are justified by reference to mandates, accountable officials should pursue lines of inquiry exploring the relative efficacy of alternative service methodologies.

"Authoritative" standards are established by legislative enactments, and pursuant regulations. Strictly speaking, legislation authorizing the provision of public services should include standards of implementation. Indeed, setting standards of service demonstrates a high order of legislative responsibility. "Accepted" standards are sanctioned by traditional practice, or technical requirements. In an outstanding example of adherence to tradition, for many decades in its history, the United States Government adopted "balanced budgets," although not required to do so by the Constitution. Widespread municipal government acceptance of fire defense specifications advocated by fire insurance interests is a good example of technical standards affecting budget allocations.   Unquestionably, state legislatures have the authority to adopt standards for the conduct of public education, and to require the adherence of accountable officials. Although they possess the right to prescribe standards for the provision of any service they authorize, legislators frequently avoid so doing, most likely to provide implementing administrators, such as, state school superintendents, with operational flexibility.

EXHIBIT 4.2 Examples of Service Standards

	MARKET EQUITY	**EQUAL EFFORT**	**EQUAL RESULTS**
EDUCATION	Per student expenditure is proportional to taxes paid.	Per student expenditure is same for all students.	Per student expenditure is variously allocated until all students achieve at, or above, minimum standards.
PUBLIC WAYS	Frequency of street cleaning is proportional to taxes paid.	Frequency of street cleaning is same for all streets.	Frequency of street cleaning varies according to the amount of litter.

As pointed up by Exhibit 4.2, *Examples of Service Standards,* methodologies express policies. Indeed, at the time of this writing, 2020, the ways and means of organizing and funding the public schools is a prime concern at all levels and branches of government in the United States.   Obviously, service standards have budgetary impacts.

It is equally obvious that expenditure classifications can help, or hinder, budgetmakers seeking to identify the budgetary effects and effects of service standards. Budget formats which focus attention on expenditure objects, such, as salaries and commodities, hide, rather than spotlight the relationship of proposed allocations to service standards. In contrast, policy and performance-oriented classifications direct attention to proposed expenditure aggregations related to service standards, as well as goals and expected results. However, as previously noted, establishing that a proposed allocation is justified by an authoritative or accepted service standard does not relieve budgetmakers of responsibility to assess its merit by applying performance criteria, especially the efficacy triad.

Performance Ratios

Producing quotients, performance ratios provide abstract measures of relationships between program investments and results. Program allocations may be expressed in terms of cost and/or work time. Results may be variously defined in terms of goals, objectives, intentions, workloads, outputs, outcomes and impacts. In budgets organized in cost center order, performance ratio calculations help budgetmakers to ration resources. In addition to stimulating initiatives to reduce the cost and/or effort of attaining objectives, considerations of performance ratios, such as the capital/labor ratio, promotes experimentation with techniques of production and technology. These features make performance ratios an important instrument of budgetary thought. The development, maintenance and application of performance measures should be actively encouraged by appropriation authorities. Data aggregation and accuracy, rather than calculation, is the chief problem in using performance ratios.

In assessing budgets for intrinsic and relative merit, appropriation authorities should demand that accountable officials actively seek to decrease the unit costs of program operations, increase output per work hour and enhance unique, favorable programmatic performance ratios. With regard to programmatic ratios, nearly all public programs are dependent, in various degrees, on scientific, professional and technical personnel. The national societies of professional and technical personnel are important sources of programmatic performance standards and criteria. Ratios published by these societies abound.

Efficiency. These ratios express the relationship of costs and/or work time to indicators of production. Unit costs are produced by dividing measurements of cost (x) by specified results (y). Units per cost is determined by the reverse procedure. Unit times are produced by dividing measure of effort by performance indicators of programmatic outputs, that is, outcomes or impacts. The reverse procedure produces work time per measure of results. In addition to describing procedures involved in the calculation of unit measures, Exhibit 4.3, *Unit Measures,* also lists a desired tendency for each type of measure.

EXHIBIT 4.3 Unit Measures

		DESIRED TENDENCY
x/y	Cost (x) per specified results (y)	Down
y/x	Specified results (y) per cost (x)	Up
z/y	Work time (z) per specified results (y)	Down
y/z	Specified results (y) per work time (z)	Up

Unit measurements are useful because they automatically relate two variables of interest, creating a third variable which facilitates comparisons. Educators compare per pupil costs; economists, output per man-hour, motorists, miles per gallon of gas. Arrayed in a time series, they facilitate objective evaluation of production techniques. Directing attention to the relationship of cost and/or work time to results helps budget-makers focus on the "production function" of budget allocations.

As a case in point, consider allocations devoted to remediation, an important educational strategy. Usually an intensive process, remediation is more expensive than standard subject-matter presentations. Assuming that the per pupil cost of remediation, provided "in-house," can be satisfactorily determined, this unit measure can then be compared to market prices for this service, and this activity assigned to a contract supplier, if the market price is favorable. One often hears of parents paying for remedial instruction, thus providing a benchmark unit cost for comparison to an "in-house" cost. One also hears about teachers teaching parents how to conduct remedial exercises for low-achieving students, a cost-effective strategy that can produce positive educational effects.

In addition to helping budgetmakers evaluate the relative merit of alternative production techniques, performance ratios facilitate program monitoring. Actual and estimated ratios can be compared to pre-set targets or standards, stimulating timely action to correct undesired deviances. Further, they can be compared to market prices for similar products, which, if more favorable, may suggest changes in production technique or decisions to "buy rather than make."

In practice, the utility of unit costs may be limited by 1) the impact of price increases, and 2) changes in the composition of costs, if the production situation remains unchanged. In both cases, an increase in unit costs has no management meaning. In this regard, consider the impact of teacher pay differentials. Public school teachers usually are compensated by pay plans which specify salary payments by time-in-service, educational attainment, and, perhaps, certain merit-related indicators. Consequently staffing costs, school-by-school and class by class, may vary significantly, depending on the variations in pay of assigned teachers. Accordingly, the unit costs of separate schools, and programs within them, may vary significantly, without shedding any light on the production situation.

Although costs, and unit costs, such as cost per pupil, are important considerations in the budgetary thinking of school officials, *time-on-task* is the most critical variable.

With regard to price increases, in periods of currency devaluation (inflation) the cost of doing business increases, causing unit costs to rise, despite managerial efforts and improvements in production technique. Obviously, this circumstance undermines the evaluation utility of unit costs, unless adjusted for inflation. Consequently, unit times are to be preferred. Unaffected by currency degradation and responsive to changes in production technique and technology, a scheme of unit times (production per work hour) is more useful and revealing, over time, than unit costs.

As isolated statistics, performance measures, provide no insight. Valid comparisons are needed to endow unit measures with policy and managerial significance. This point is illustrated by Exhibit 4.4, *Time Series Comparison of Unit Cost.* This indicative Exhibit assumes that a school system has invested $100,000 in its truancy program. This cost includes direct variable charges, such as, salaries, supplies, etc., but excludes indirect fixed charges, such as, overhead costs, vehicle depreciation, etc. The accountable staff serviced 400 cases, at a unit cost of $250.00 per case. The Exhibit displays the effect of trying to decrease truancy by addressing "precursor" symptoms and "causal" variables with remedial action. The current year implementation of this effort temporarily increases the unit cost. However, the budget for the upcoming year reflects the desired effect of the initiative on costs, cases and unit cost.

EXHIBIT 4.4 Time Series Comparison of Unit Costs

TRUANCY PROGRAM	LAST YEAR	THIS YEAR	BUDGET
Investment (Variable Cost)	$100,000	$110,000	$60,000
Number of Cases	400.	350	250
Cost per Case	$250.00	$314.29	$240.00

As illustrated by Exhibit 4.4, *Time Series Comparison of Unit Costs*, unit measures can be compared in a time series. They may also be compared to standard costs, that is, expected unit costs set up during the budget preparation period. If suppliers are available, they can be matched to market prices. Most important from a budgetary perspective, they can be compared in a series of production situations involving different levels of investment, production techniques and estimated performance. Time series unit measure comparisons, similar to that shown in Exhibit 4.4, are frequently employed in the formulation of solution-centered, results-oriented budgets.

At this point, it is prudent to point out the protean nature of the term, "cost." Budgets and financial statements display "cost" data. This data can be displayed in sundry ways, reflecting different conceptions of "cost," School budgets may be based on "cash," that is, receipts and disbursements expected during a given fiscal period. To enhance budget control, outstanding commitments may be added to disbursements, a practice known as modified accrual accounting. The resulting costs are called expenditures. Under full accrual accounting, costs are called expenses. Finally, depending on one's purpose, costs may be defined as direct, variable, controllable, indirect, fixed, total, standard, unit, sunk or marginal.

Significantly, cost arrays are not neutral. Like budgetary classifications, cost definitions affect thinking and decisions. Characteristically, budget documents identify costs as 1) "direct/variable" and 2) "indirect/fixed." Typically, public school budgets are a composite of direct/variable and indirect/fixed costs.

Costs identified as direct/variable are those that vary consistently with measures of production, (classroom instruction, for example). If workload and/or output rises, direct/variable costs (wages, supplies, etc.) may also be expected to rise. If falling, so should variable costs. In management theory, by deriving a unit cost for those costs which vary directly with measures of production, program staff can be held accountable for costs at different production volumes. Costs that are identified as indirect/fixed are those which are logically, but "indirectly," associated with specific production situations (cost for central process units, for example).

By their very nature, indirect/fixed costs do not vary with fluctuations of specific production situations. Seeking "total" costs, indirect/fixed costs may be derived and assigned to specific production situations by applying arbitrary distribution formulas. For example, proportionate shares of administrative "overhead" costs may be distributed to various cost centers by the relative employee effort assigned to each. As a rule, indirect/fixed costs do not fluctuate with production characteristics over the short run. However, significant shifts in production situations over a period of time may affect the amount of staff, space, equipment, and other fixed charges which are assigned to an activity.

In general, it is unwise to maintain unit measures at high levels of aggregation, as this may hide, rather than highlight, opportunities for a series of minor changes in procedure which can add up to an impressive productivity improvement.

To successfully implement a scheme of unit measures, one needs to identify an output indicator for each cost center, or vice versa, set up a cost center for each output indicator. Obviously, each indicator must be discrete, and amenable to accurate tabulation. Each investment pattern has its own appropriate measures of performance (MOP) which should be formally described and entered into an accounting record.

School officials find it relatively easy to apply unit cost criteria to auxiliary services and "business" operations, such as, plant maintenance, printing services, transportation, etc. In these cases, one usually has established accurate costs and well-understood performance measures. *Ceteris paribus,* the unit measures of classroom instruction will vary with the wages of the assigned staff, as compensation scales vary with time-in-service and educational attainments. Under these conditions, unit cost comparisons of schools and classrooms are not, on their face, of budgetary significance. But, unit measures, based on time-on-task data, might have significant budgetary implications.

It is not as easy, however, to apply unit cost criteria to strictly "educational" investments. In addition to problematic estimates, school officials calculating the unit costs of educational activities must cope with controversy over performance measures. "Cost per student" is probably the most popular unit measure of educational expenditure. However, this unit of measurement is frequently cast at high, rather than low levels of expenditure aggregation, such as, elementary education cost per pupil, secondary education cost per pupil, and per pupil cost, system-wide. Student cost calculations seem far less common at lower levels of aggregation, such as, subject matter units, or curriculum tracks. One suspects that school officials wishing to use unit measures at these lower levels of aggregation are inhibited by accounting deficiencies, principally the failure to record, and report, the deployment of student and teacher time.

If school systems maintain cost records by school, educational authorities can, and should, explore per pupil cost variations among comparable units. These cost aggregations should include direct costs, and a rationalized distribution of indirect costs. School authorities should seek "explanations," in operational terms, of school-to-school differences. Comparisons are always fruitful, particularly if these probes search for correlations between investment and student achievement and attainment. Also, applying the literary criterion to budgets, these school-by-school statistics should be an integral part of documentation made public. This publication requirement encourages school authorities to undertake the recommended exploration.

All public school systems should aggregate and report school-by-school costs. A comparative analysis of these cost aggregations can be very productive. The budgetmaker's toolbox may well include graphic arrays such as that displayed by Appendix B, *Per-Pupil Costs Related to School Size*.

The scattergram displayed in Appendix B points up the cost implications of school scale. The scatter shown in this graphic display also serves to provoke questions about expenditure variations which cannot be explained by the influence of scale. They deepen thought, provoke inquiry, stimulate fact-finding, and provide effective vehicles for communicating budget issues and proposals.

How much of the observed variation is "caused" by different curricula, by pay differentials due to teacher assignment practices, or by school idiosyncrasies, such as, relative plant efficiencies, etc.? And what about achievement and attainment, the most important questions of all?. Are unit cost variations related to measures of performance? Most assuredly, per-pupil expenditure cannot be considered an unqualified "causal" variable in public school funding.

To explore the relationships between per-pupil costs and student performance, school officials must assemble cost and performance data at appropriate checkpoints, within and across schools and curricula. The performance database includes a diverse array of statistics, such as, test scores, grade movement data, attendance rates, graduation rates, etc. For example, the latest testing data in reading can be aggregated by school, and then related to costs per student. A provocative set of comparisons may result. They compel the budgetmaker's mind, willing or not, to contemplate the causes and components of school productivity (staff and leadership qualities, teaching techniques, student time deployments, capital/labor ratios, etc.), weighing the influence of each on student achievement and attainment. In this connection, one recalls the findings of the Colman Report regarding the weak correlation of many conventional "causal" variables with student performance, except the verbal facility of teachers.

Unit measures stimulate thinking, and thereby illuminate opportunities for action. These powerful media of budgetary evaluation belong in every budgetmaker's toolbox. Use them!

One final note of caution before we proceed. The comparative value of unit costs is significantly reduced during periods of currency inflation. One can combat this by applying "price deflators" to the data. Of course, this procedure, while excellent, increases the burden of calculation. Maintaining productivity records which relate work hours to output measures (unit times) is another way to avoid the distorting influence of currency inflation. Furthermore, unit times are particularly good for monitoring productivity trends in labor-intensive programs.

Effectiveness. Ratios which relate performance measurements to targets are particularly valuable as they testify to program effectiveness. For example, 1,000 high school students are enrolled in 10th grade classes. Two years later, 800 of these students graduate. Dividing the number graduating by the original 10th grade cohort produces an effectiveness ratio of 80%, leaving a performance gap of 20%. Proposals to increase effectiveness ratios (or close performance gaps) deserve close scrutiny as performance improvements are usually harder (and more costly) to obtain as effectiveness ratios near 100% — an effect well known as "diminishing returns." This aside, budget documentation referencing effectiveness ratios certainly provide a good starting point for an assessment of the relative merit of proposed allocations.

The performance ratio concepts thus far discussed can be applied generally. The last ratio concept identifies proportions that are programmatically specific. Programmatic ratios take on budgetary significance when they are used as references for the evaluation of current or proposed practice.

Programmatic. The well-known pupil/teacher ratio is an example of a relationship concept specific to education programming. In assessing education allocations, this ratio is given considerable weight by those interested in financial policy.

As previously noted, the national societies of professional and technical personnel are important sources of programmatic performance standards and criteria. The National Center for Education Statistics is a source of programmatic data. For example, it tracks the ratio of students with access to instructional computers, certainly a relationship of great concern to educational authorities. The Center also tracks the ratio of library volumes per student.

Reference to programmatic ratios, capital/labor ratios, for example, serve to enrich budgetary thought. Beyond doubt, the calculation and display of capital/labor ratios directs attention to production techniques and technology, especially when services heavily dependent on personal services are under consideration. Judicially applied, with allowance for particular circumstances, budgetmakers can, and should, use programmatic ratios to evaluate the substance and thrust of programs under review.

In sum, the introduction and maintenance of a scheme of performance ratios helps to ensure that investments are correlated with workloads and goals. Most important, a comprehensive scheme of performance ratios makes it difficult for accountable officials to shun responsibility for productivity improvements. All educators who supervise the work of others should justify their production decisions by reference to the values of the efficacy triad, that is, effectiveness, efficiency and economy. This injunction also applies to teachers, who must manage their own time, and more important, the time-on-task of their students.

Modeling

At the beginning of this discussion about the budgetmaker's toolbox, I pointed out that a budget's "production function" can be described by the general equation, y = f(x). Revisiting this conception re-enforces the idea that mathematics, especially mathematical modeling, can (and should) be used to illuminate educational programming and budgeting. As the reader will recall, in this equation, "x" equals the allocated resources, "y" equals output/outcome/impact, quantified, if possible, if not, then specified verbally. and "f" symbolically denotes the production technique, such as, instruction, drill and practice, homework, etc. It was also pointed out that this equation assumes that changes in applied resources produce corresponding changes in programmatic effects and affects—a linear conception of the budgeting process, accurate within limits. In most cases, however, the relationship between resources applied and results is not constant, and is better described by curvilinear, rather than linear conceptions of cause and consequence. This important idea is considered in detail in the upcoming discussion of marginal productivity.

Multivariate mathematical modeling is applicable because, more often than not, educational programs are complex activities. A well-known example comes readily to mind: the dual function of the elementary and secondary schools, simultaneously providing "education" and "daycare" services, depending on one's viewpoint. One could advance more examples of causation and multiple effects in public safety, public health and other complex programs. Although mathematical relationships, i.e., performance ratios, provide valuable insights into questions about the relative merit of budget allocations, accountable officials also need a way to explore complex programs. Appropriation authorities charged with assessing the intrinsic merit of proposed allocations for complex programs, can enrich the review process by asking accountable program staff to identify the relative impact of different production variables on a desired result, an application of the concept of mathematical modeling.

School budgets are usually built up, bit by bit, program by program. To be sure, this process of aggregation produces certain benefits, such as, responsible (but not necessarily accurate) estimates, expenditure documentation, orderly reviews, etc. The process has, however, a major drawback: It tends to immerse budgetmakers in detail ("drown" is perhaps a better word), making it hard to get and keep a "sense-of-the-whole." Broad perspectives are very important in budget work, especially at adoption time. Indeed, budgetmakers who cannot maintain an adequate conception of overall mission and effectiveness are forced to specialize in trivia, suffering impaired judgment and reduced relevance in the bargain.

As all budgetmakers know, it is not easy to rise above the flood of minutiae. In addition to a strong resolve, a commitment to "modeling" can help. In order to model, budgetmakers must first slice through masses of facts and values to isolate those few key variables which "make a difference" in system performance, that is, control the ability of the system to achieve its master goal(s). If they can then specify the relationship of these key variables to one another, and to the goal(s), they will be in position to construct and use models in the budgetary process.

Best described as hypothetical statements, models involve an ordered set of assumptions about causes, effects, and objectives. Models can be elaborate, but not necessarily so. See Appendix C, *An Indicative Illustration of Modeling Procedures,* for a sample application of modeling focused on variables thought to affect learning reading by third grade students.

The educational process includes many events which can be profitably treated as "variables" subject to correlation studies. The decision of students to "drop out" provides a case in point. Society invests in the compulsory education of students who then leave school short of high school graduation. The social and personal costs of "dropping out" are unknown, but are estimated to be many times the educational investment. The decision to "drop out" has precursors, which include outside-school (socio-economic) and in-school variables. Relevant in-school markers are a) weak acquisition of school-based skills of mathematics and language, b) frequent absences, c) failing grades and d) inappropriate behavior. The relative influence of these variables can be assessed by means of multivariate correlations, and directly addressed with targeted resource allocations. Importantly, this approach provides a strong basis for monitoring results. See Appendix D, *"Dropout" Reduction: An Indicative Illustration of Performance Budget Analysis and Documentation,* for a sample application of modeling focused on the high school "dropout" problem.

Computers have put mathematical modeling within easy reach of public officials, done in-house or commercially. (One could and should engage the interest and talent of high school mathematics teachers and students in budget-related modeling, paying the students.) Such systematic correlation studies illuminate the relative effects of variables thought to influence programmatic performance. Models define an ordered set of assumptions about causes, effects and objectives. By using models to specify relationships between variables thought to "make a difference," public officials can better advance their ability to attain and sustain a desired level of effectiveness. As hypothetical statements, models display an ordered set of assumptions about causes, effects and objectives.

Summing up, the abstract nature of models encourages us to concentrate on important and effective variables, to the exclusion of all else. This is an immense advantage for budgetmakers, who are frequently distracted by peripheral issues and administrative trivia. Models belong in every budgetmaker's toolbox. Build them and use them!

Investment Returns

School officials applying investment criteria to allocation decisions are likely to gain valuable insights into the opportunity costs of various educational strategies. Given the limitation on in-school learning hours, the assignment of teacher and student time is the most important allocation issue, evidenced by reliance on "homework" as a costless way to expand student time-on-task. Consequently, it is. deemed axiomatic that different deployments of teacher and student time-on-task produce different educational benefits. However, as will be noted below, although theoretically valuable, calculation difficulties limit application of investment return comparisons in practice.

Investment Yield. It is fair to say that appropriation authorities assume, usually on subjective grounds, that their expenditure authorizations will produce "benefits" equaling or exceeding their cost, including an allowance for interest. It is also fair to say that they assume that their authorized programs and projects produce more "benefit" than other possible investments —that, in effect, there is no "opportunity cost" associated with their authorizations. In pure theory, the intrinsic and relative merit of programs and projects depend on comparative "rate of return" calculations.

Insight into intrinsic merit may be gained by dividing the estimated monetized benefit conferred by a program or project by its estimated cost, expressed as a ratio, or as a percentage. To quality as a viable investment, the benefit/cost ratio must exceed 1 plus an assumed interest percentage. The calculation can also be expressed as a percentage. Insight into relative merit may be gained by ranking proposed programs and projects by investment returns.

With dedicated effort, estimated benefits can be ascribed, and possibly monetized, for programs where price-based comparisons are available, e.g., private schools, remedial services and internet-provided courses. When people are willing to pay for goods and services, they are monetizing their values. Although such comparative data must be used with care, budgetmakers will find it rewarding to assemble and use information about free-market analogies to explore the merit of proposed allocations.

To apply investment criteria, as suggested, budgetmakers must develop and maintain a suitable database. Experts on the subject suggest that the public's *willingness to pay*, as distinguished from ability to pay, is the surest index of benefit. This data may be gleaned from private market prices for services analogous to public school services such as the price for private schooling, tutoring, exam preparation, etc.

Establishing service charges, or polling users of public services on their willingness to pay, are two ways to garner data on benefits. Cost avoidance, or savings, ascribed to investments are also legitimately included in benefit calculations. Further, benefits can be described as positive (+ but ?), or negative (- but ?), if the tendency is known, but the benefit cannot be accurately estimated. See Appendix A, *An Annotated Model Published Budget*, for an example of the use of this symbolic technique.

EXHIBIT 4.5 Investment Return Comparisons

	Gross Benefit	Total Investment	Net Benefit	Return
Program X	150,000	125,000	25,000	20%
Program Y	125,000	81,250	43.750	35%
Program Z	100,000	50,000	50,000	50%

With these measures in hand, the proposed allocations in question can be comparatively considered for adoption. Indicative Exhibit 4.5, *Investment Return Comparisons,* shows how an array of programs might be compared by means of the return on investment criterion. Referring to the exhibit, if the minimum acceptable rate of return is set at 25%, representing the "admissibility" criterion, funding of Program X would not be justified, unless it could be redesigned to improve its return.

Using such comparisons, budgetmakers may select an array of programs which can produce the highest overall return for a given expenditure level. Proving that a budget proposal meets the basic admissibility criterion is, in itself, a major burden for budgetmakers, to say nothing of the analytical burdens which confront them when they try to apply investment criteria to evaluate the relative merits of a spectrum of proposals.

This brief reconnaissance cannot do justice to the technical refinements and qualifications which condition the application of the investment yield criterion, such as the effects of time and interest rates. While technical problems are formidable, it is the issues surrounding benefit estimation which make the investment criterion difficult to apply. Unless budgetmakers can develop accepted methods for the estimation of program benefits, this deficiency will continue to inhibit the application of the investment yield criterion

In those cases where benefits cannot be monetized, making the preferred benefit/cost approach impossible, yet results can be numerically specified, budgetmakers may apply a cost/effectiveness approach. Also, as noted below in the discussion of marginal productivity, lacking a common denominator, the estimated results of disparate programs cannot be objectively compared. However, the changes can, be rendered comparable if converted to percentages, providing a common denominator for comparisons. Weighting and scoring schemes, discussed shortly, provide another way to gain insight into comparative values.

Marginal Productivity. In considering the possibilities of goal displacement and means substitution one must estimate where programs stand in terms of marginal productivity.

Exhibit 4.6 Lazy "S" Curve

Exhibit 4.6, *Lazy "S" Curve,* presents a graphic representation of a curve describing the concept of "diminishing returns."

Assuming a stable mix of resources and production techniques, the curve describes relatively low program efficacy at low levels of expenditure (x), sharp increases in benefits (y) as expenditure rises, but a declining rate for increased expenditure thereafter. . At the top of the curve, this situation is analogous to the "saturated market" of private enterprise. The concept of the "lazy 'S' curve" can be helpful in the following two ways:

First, budgetmakers thinking in terms of the curve are encouraged to describe and evaluate the relationship between the inputs and results of different investments with a single end.

Providing an indicative example, Exhibit 4.7, *Diminishing Returns,* assumes alternative deployments of student time-on-task devoted to the mastery of mathematics, requiring 25, 30 and 35 percent of class time available for instruction.

Exhibit 4.7 Diminishing Returns.

STRATEGY	ACHIEVEMENT
25% Deployment	70%
30% Deployment	80%
35% Deployment	85%

Achievement is stated in terms of the percentage of students scoring above a set standard on "criterion-based" tests. Each deployment yields a higher achievement, but at a declining rate, suggesting that increasing investment of student time-on-task has progressively less justification. On the other hand, budgetmakers should look approvingly on proposed allocations associated with rising marginal productivity when performance is below the margin, the inflection point on the curve. In those cases, It would be appropriate to suggest that resources be augmented by transfer from programs where it is found that the allocations are associated with diminishing productivity.

Second, budgetmakers thinking in terms of the curve of marginal productivity are encouraged to compare input/results relationships of investments aimed at different ends, such as mathematics versus reading competency of elementary school children. This problem is usually dismissed "out-of-hand", as one cannot compare things or events that lack a common denominator, "apples compared to oranges," as the popular saying goes. However, when changes in input/results relationships are expressed as percentages, these ratios can be usefully compared. Thus, budgetmakers can apply the concept of the "lazy 'S' curve" to locate and recommend resource transfers from programs with the lowest rates of change to those offering higher rates.

Because time is the key educational resource, exploring the marginal productivity of time-on-task deployments is strongly recommended, especially for budgets for schools marked by low achievement in the mastery of basic skills. Most certainly, the chief cause of waste in using budgetary resources is the under and ineffective utilization of time-on-task ostensibly allocated for the mastery of basic skills. The marginal effect on achievement by lengthening actual (rather than nominal) time-on-task by, let us say, 5, 10 or 15 minutes can be plotted, and the point of diminishing returns established.

Thinking in terms of marginal productivity tends to alert budgetmakers to possibilities for goal displacement and/or means substitution, two ways to make allocation changes that strengthen overall budgetary efficacy. *The disposition to relentlessly pursue opportunities for goal displacement and means substitution is a distinguishing mark of competent budgetmakers.*

Weighting and Scoring

Budgetmakers who despair of applying investment criteria can turn to weighting and scoring procedures to help illuminate the comparative worth of competitive proposals.

Ordinal Ranking. The simplest and most popular prioritization technique produces a priority list by requiring budgetmakers to rank allocation proposals by assigning numbers 1, 2, 3, etc., meaning "first," "second," "third." The letters A, B, C, etc. are also used to assign priority. These numbers or letters frequently represent the application of defined prioritization concepts, such as, urgent, essential, required, necessary, desirable, etc. Proposals may be sorted into broad priority categories, such as, high, medium, low, and then given an ordinal rank within each group. Ordinal rankings may be assigned by individuals, or groups, using agreed-upon criteria and decision rules. In passing, it is worth noting that ordinal ranking procedures are a key feature of Zero-Base Budgeting (ZBB).

Multi-Dimensional Scoring. Comparative values can also be established by using weighting and scoring procedures. Weights may be assigned by individuals, or better yet, groups applying agreed upon criteria and decision rules. Scoring procedures are required when proposals are assigned two or more priority designations. In this procedure, priority scores are assigned to proposals by reference to a table of values. Although there is no magic in weighting and scoring procedures, budgetmakers use them to clarify the subjective judgments influencing budget allocations.

Establishing a weighting and scoring matrix provides an important benefit to participants in the exercise. The procedure encourages the clarification of values. To explore this effect, consider the assumptions of Exhibit 4.8, *Weighting and Scoring Model.*

EXHIBIT 4.8 Weighting and Scoring Model

Concerns		Legally Prescribed	Improve Results	Maintain Program	Enrich Offerings
	Priority	0	1	2	3
Health & Safety	1	0	1	2	3
Pre-School	2	0	2	4	6
Primary	3	0	3	6	9
Secondary	4	0	4	8	12
Extra-Curricular	5	0	5	10	15

This model assumes that the accountable officials have agreed on two ordinal scales, with zero assigned to "mandated" programs and services. Assigning zero to mandated proposals puts them at the top of the list, regardless of other considerations. With this exception, budget allocations can be tested against the values of the priority scheme, and its comparative rank established.

The vertical scale of prioritized concerns also assumes that the value of formal education is highest in the early years of child development, declining as students age. Although it assumes that results are the transcendent priority, the horizontal scale indicates that program continuity outranks innovation. Illustrating use of the matrix, a proposal concerning the health and safety of students would draw a "1" from a list expressing the school authority's concerns. As the proposal might be deemed to improve results, it draws a "1" from the list of allocation criteria, earning a total score of "1," the highest priority. .

In another example, a proposal to enrich the program of extracurricular activities would draw a "5" as a school authority concern, and a "3" from its list of allocation priorities. Multiplying these numbers produces a priority score of "15," the lowest priority. Following this procedure, proposed allocations, can be assigned to an appropriate group with a rank number from zero (mandated) to "15." This methodology requires that expenditure proposals be aggregated by cost in priority group order until a selected expenditure total is reached. When the aggregation exceeds the desired limit, proposals in the affected priority group can be again prioritized to determine which, if any, will be included in the aggregate budget.

Obviously, weighting and scoring schemes organize, rather than eliminate, the subjective judgments of those involved in the budget process. This, however, is a major benefit because the establishment of the scheme itself encourages budgetmakers, and other participants to clarify and "objectify" their values.

To conclude this discussion of the budgetmaker's toolbox, the effort to assess the intrinsic and relative merit of allocations helps to spotlight opportunities to displace program goals and/or substitute program procedures. It is widely acknowledged that public programs, and their procedures, tend to roll on, unchallenged and essentially unchanged, from year to year. In the heavily-weighted inertial environment of government bureaucracies, budgetmakers should aggressively promote the concept of ***goal displacement and means substitution.*** This is important work, as redirecting allocations from ineffective and/or inefficient programs to new initiatives enables governments to address new problems without additional taxes or loans. As noted above, and repeated here for emphasis, "The disposition to relentlessly pursue opportunities for goal displacement and means substitution is a distinguishing mark of competent budgetmakers."

Key Thoughts in Review

Whenever possible, educational investments should be related to results by means of objective measures.

Unit costs acquire policy and management meaning when compared, *certeris parabus*, to standard costs, to market prices and when arrayed in a time series.

Per-pupil costs are of limited value, unless related to measures of student achievement and attainment.

In order to avoid the distorting effects of inflation on unit costs, and to probe the production techniques of labor-intensive programs, budgetmakers are advised to establish an array of unit times.

Budgetmakers pondering the behavior of unit measures pay attention to production techniques and the impact of technology.

Although applications are limited by lack of benefit data, budgetmakers are urged to seek investment return comparisons to assess the relative merit of selected allocations.

Budgetmakers applying the concept of "diminishing returns" also tend to think about the opportunity gains and losses of any given deployment of student and faculty time.

After a certain point, educational investments produce less and less benefit, an example of diminishing returns.

The disposition to relentlessly pursue opportunities for goal displacement and means substitution is a distinguishing mark of competent budgetmakers.

5. Preliminary Work

... the ways, means and benefits of anticipatory thinking about future budgets.

At a certain point in the fiscal year, school officials begin serious thinking about next year's budget. This forward thinking includes various forms of budget anticipation and planning, if only to update forms and instructions defining the formulation and documentation process. As a formal matter, the process is usually initiated by issuance of a "call for estimates," accompanied by forms and instructions. Ideally, prior to issuance, the accountable administrative and program staff have done "front-end" thinking, resulting in the formulation of a fiscal and budgetary perspective.

Most certainly, anticipatory thinking and action should provide estimates of financial capability, including pro forma estimates of current year revenues and expenditures and year-end fund balances. In the critical programmatic dimension, anticipatory efforts should identify the issues, problems and opportunities facing the school district, outlining potential solutions. To be conducted effectively, a district-wide anticipatory process requires a sharply focused, vigorously managed research program, best conducted by a broad-based team appointed by the district's chief administrator. As key participants, principals should conduct school-by-school anticipatory processes.

These and other forms of anticipatory thinking and action can (and should) be welded into a cohesive fiscal and budgetary perspective. When issued, the instructions incorporated in the "call for estimates" should reference the findings of this perspective.

As suggested by Exhibit 5.1, *Elements of an Anticipatory Process*, organizational arrangements include administrative support drawn from the district's finance establishment, serving as a secretariat for the district-wide process. At this stage of budget formulation, documentation of problem-solving initiatives need only be detailed to the extent required to establish them as candidates for consideration in the upcoming budget.

EXHIBIT 5.1 Elements of an Anticipatory Process

ORGANIZATIONAL REQUIREMENTS
  Adopt a research agenda, initiating the budget cycle.
  Specify role and responsibilities of research teams.
  Assign. financial staff to serve as secretariat.
  Communicate and document, stressing consultation,
    clearance, disclosure and transparency.
  Control the research process, relying on dynamic monitoring.

PROCESS

  Survey Issues, Problems and Opportunities
    Conduct Public Forums
    Convene Technical Conferences
    Commission Technical Papers

  . . .

  Formulate and Document Financial Capability
    Estimate resources and formulate Mobilization Methodology
    Formulate a Multi-year Financial Capability Statement/

  Formulate and Document Proposed Initiatives
    Select Key Issues, Problems and Opportunities
    Formulate proposed initiatives, using the following format:
      Define program rationale
      State goal(s) in a multiyear perspective
      Identify collaborators and affected parties
      Identify conditions required for goal attainment
      Formulate preferred solution(s) and tentative work plan(s)
      Formulate tentative multi-year budget
      Identify alternatives considered and rationale for rejection.

  Complete and Submit Fiscal & Budgetary Perspective

Reflecting the intrinsic difficulties of prediction, a weak, haphazard approach to anticipating future events will surely waste time and resources, and, quite probably will have regrettable consequences. Anticipatory thinking and action confer the following advantages:

- The formulation of fiscal and budgetary perspectives tends to promote organizational cohesion by improving communication.

- The educational impacts of thoughtful perspectives on officials and other interested and affected parties can be significant. Indeed, this potential effect provides the effort to formulate perspectives with sufficient rationale.

However, the strongest rationale for establishing an anticipatory organization and process lies in its stimulation of decision-related research. The anticipatory process outlined by Exhibit 5.1 features discussion and reflection on complex matters by qualified parties. As noted, the process of developing perspectives begins with an assessment of issues, problems and opportunities, conducted by means of public forums, technical conferences and technical papers—a process designed to encourage the vigorous participation of non-politicized, non-bureaucratized parties. Generally, participants will find an anticipatory process stimulating.

As recommended herein, fiscal and budgetary perspectives reflect the results of organized thinking about the efficacy of present and possible future policies and programs. Beyond providing a basis for the formulation of budget proposals, their prime purpose, perspectives inform the thinking of all interested parties, especially educational policy-makers.

In sum, what outcome justifies an investment of a jurisdiction's resources in the development of an annual fiscal and budgetary perspective? Effective implementation of efficacious programs and projects is the short answer to this important question.

Key Thoughts in Review

Well before the onset of the next fiscal year, the district's accountable administrative and program staff should engage in systematic "front-end" thinking, resulting in the formulation of a fiscal and budgetary perspective.

The strongest rationale for establishing an anticipatory organization and process lies in its stimulation of decision-related research.

6. Formulation and Documentation

...sets forth a scheme of seven topics to be addressed by administrative and program officials when formulating and documenting proposed budget allocations.

As numbers, budgets provide the price of programmatic requirements. Logically, however, desired programmatic results should be the primary consideration of budgetmakers, with pricing of requirements an associated concern. In practice, budgets evolve, reflecting an interplay of programmatic desires with the consciousness of financial constraints. In best practice, the process encourages the formulation of allocations justified by the principled application of evidence and logic to the key task of budget appraisal: the determination of the intrinsic and relative merit of proposed allocations of public funds. Requiring proposers to address a sequence of prescribed topics ensures a uniform and efficacious approach to this challenging task.

Who should have responsibility for originating budget proposals?. This is a significant question, with significant implications. As commonly perceived, public school districts provide facilities, comprising production units (classrooms) distributed at the base of a hierarchy, supported by the services of an array of centralized process agencies. Long-term trends favoring departmentalization have increased organizational complexity and the means of centralized control. In many districts, budget formulation and documentation procedures are substantially in the hands of key administrators. In an apropos remark, a business manager of a large urban district reportedly said, "given enrollment projections, I can make up the district budget in a closet."

If implemented, the recommendations outlined in Part 3, *Administrative and Accounting Foundations,* would strengthen the budgetary role of principals and teachers at the base of the hierarchy. Clearly, as "headmasters" (an out-of-favor title suggesting scholarly attributes), school principals are likely budgetmakers of first instance.

Exhibit 6.1 Budget Formulation and Documentation

	STATEMENT	SPECIFICATIONS
1	RATIONALE	A concise statement of the perplexities to be addressed, defined as issues, problems and opportunities justifying the budget. Identifies causal relationships (correlations) between key variables and desired results. Presents the preferred solution.
2	GOAL(S)	As targets, performance indicators are defined in practical, measurable, time-bound terms.
3	COLLABORATORS AND AFFECTED PARTIES	In addition to parties (or units) providing (upstream) or receiving (downstream) assistance from the unit in question, identifies those to be served and/or regulated by the proposed activities, providing insight into the conferred benefits.
4	CONDITIONS OF PERFORMANCE	Description of factors required to produce goal attainment. These include institutional aspects (organization, procedures, staff capability, regulations, procedures, equipment, etc.), and most important, the assumptions and standards which influence the size, shape, direction and feasibility of the proposed programmatic solution to the situation described in Statement #1.
5	WORK PLAN (Preferred Solution)	An annotated Work Plan implementing the preferred solution to the situation described in Statement 1. The plan provides a matrix, listing activities or tasks, assigned work hours allocated by time periods or milestones, and pertinent performance data, including ratios, such as output per work hour or unit costs. The notes provide a commentary relating the planned work to Statements 1, 2 and 3.
6	BUDGET	Supporting the preferred solution, a proposed budget (balanced by revenue) displays cost centers, performance data and interpretation.
7	ALTERNATIVES	A concise description of programmatic options considered, but rejected in favor of a preferred solution, and the reasons why. Highlights the criteria applied to justify the budget.

Further. to strengthen the budgetary role of principals, budgets should be allocated to each school as "lump sums," with principals given re-allotment rights during budget implementation. Likewise, all supervisors of central process agencies should formulate and document proposed allocations, following the procedures herein recommended.

Presenting a comprehensive methodology for crafting proposed allocations, Exhibit 6.1, *Budget Formulation and Documentation*, lists seven inter-related topics. In addressing these topics, especially Statement 1, Rationale, the following preliminary steps are recommended. Begin work with a questioning cast of mind, employing broad survey techniques to loosen up thinking.

> Review pertinent data in files and documents, especially student data.

> Review relevant literature.

> Conduct site visits, where and when appropriate.

> Consult with people who can provide insight and advice.

These gestalt-establishing steps help define relevant perplexities (issues, problems, and opportunities), the relative significance of evidence at hand, and that which must be assembled and assessed. These steps will also help ensure that the special nomenclature of the science, technology and techniques involved in the program situation are used appropriately.

Requiring "decision-related" research, the first four topics listed in Exhibit 6.1 comprise the diagnostic phase of the recommended budget formulation and documentation process. The research effort must be broad and deep enough to identify "controlling variables" and associated evidence concerning the perplexities to be addressed. A caution is in order here. Conventional or obvious statements about perplexities rooted in the student's environment are to be regarded with deep suspicion, lest they be lead to dwelling on symptoms, or worse, erroneous questions. As a case in point: Educational authorities cannot directly attack social variables, such as family dis-function, poverty and drug use, even though their effects on learning are known, and pernicious. Although they may be accurate, such variables are worthless as controlling variables. Indeed, consideration of such variables tends to excuse, rather than encourage a search for learning-causative variables which can be dynamically employed in programs designed to produce student performance.

Statement 1, Rationale

Identifying "controlling variables" is the key step in a budget formulation and documentation process. Causal relationships, or correlations, are particularly important. For example, suppose a review of student performance turns up evidence that students who change schools (due to residence change) do less well than students who do not. This correlation should influence assignment procedures for students changing residence and thus may affect the transportation budget. In another example, students are known to perform better if they receive comments on their work. Performance feedback is known to have positive effects on achievement. Shouldn't budgets reflect explicit commitments to take advantage of this "causal" concept? In yet a third example, the Colman Report indicated that the verbal facility of teachers correlates with student achievement. Shouldn't recruitment practices, pay plans and budgets express support for this "controlling" variable in the educational process?

The definition of perplexities logically influences the choice of goals(s), the specification of performance criteria and program design. Additionally, budgetmakers should assess the demographic and logistical characteristics of the situation. Who, what, why, where, when and how questions deeply intrude into all aspects of programming. Further, it is especially important to remember that. implementation is the "Achilles' Heel" of all policies and plans. To that end, the means of implementation requires serious consideration during the diagnostic phase of budget formulation.

Statement 2, Goal(s)

As a general rule, avoid completely verbal goal statements, such as, "improve the quality of education." Try instead to frame goal statements in numerical terms, such as, "Increase the proportion of 10th graders who graduate two years hence from the current ratio of

____% to ____%. In addition, setting goals in a numerical way tends to ensure that chosen goals are practical, and measurable. A goal, to be practical, must be attainable in a specific time. Remember, success in implementation is directly related to choosing goals that are practical, that is, attainable. Furthermore, if the chosen goal is measurable, it is easier to set milestones, or performance check points, which are an essential part of work plans and essential for the process of "dynamic" monitoring.

Statement 3, Collaborators and Affected Parties

Every program has a clientele, willing or not. An accurate description of collaborators and affected parties lends precision to goal statements. Target groups comprise those individuals, organized or not, perhaps even unborn, who are to be affected by the expenditures outlined in financial projections. Because an assessment of impacts and benefits depends on a description of program clientele, it pays to be as accurate as possible in identifying affected parties. Nevertheless, as advised by Aristotle in his Nicomachean Ethics, (W. D. Ross translation) more precision than the situation allows is not to be expected. Identification of collaborators is helpful in selecting participants in performance review sessions, as will be discussed later on. .

Statements 4, Conditions of Performance

Describes key factors required for goal attainment. Performance criteria include the leading ideas, the causal relationships, the assumptions, and the standards which influence the size, shape and direction of a proposed program. For example, protecting the privacy, dignity and the independence of students should be important criteria to be considered in evaluating alternative ways of improving educational performance. Working closely with parents might be another performance condition. Remember that correlations, or causal relationships, provide the firmest foundation for program planning and implementation.

Statement 5, Work Plan (Preferred Solution)

With diagnostic conclusions in hand, and written, budgetmakers are ready to determine the best way to attain stated goal(s). All who supervise the work of others, including, most critically, teachers, should formulate work plans. If diagnostic considerations form the soul of budgets, work plans supply their heart. They justify budgets because attaining a desired future takes "managerial muscle." In addition to providing "milestones" registering progress during the process of implementation, work plans provide indispensable references for effective performance reviews.

EXHIBIT 6.2 A Simplified Work Plan Model

		Periods				
	Performance Element	1	2	3	4	Total

1 Activity/Task—Work Hours
Cost
Output/Outcome/Impact
Performance Ratio
    Etc.

N Activity/Task—Work Hours
Cost
Output/Outcome/Impact
Performance Ratio
    Etc.

Total Work Hours

Authorized Absences—Hours

Total Paid Hours

Visualized as supervisors of student time-on-task, teachers should formulate and execute work plans. Further, it is simply good pedagogy to engage students and parents in work planning. Three-party planning that engages students, parents and teachers in a common enterprise, creates and sustains a learning atmosphere and student commitment to goal attainment. At this point, it is appropriated to discuss the utility of providing students with "how to study" guidance repeatedly, in every grade. This should include acquainting students with the plan of studies for that grade and beyond. Providing students with a "gestalt" endows the allotments of time-on-task with purpose and meaning.

As shown by Exhibit 6.2, *A Simplified Work Plan Model*, work plans may display data discretely, period by period, providing totals in the last column at the right. As an alternative, one may display data cumulatively, with each period's data added to the prior period. Consequently, each period provides a year-to-date total, with the last period's figures also serving as the year-end total. If desired, both formats, the discrete periodic totals and the cumulative year-to-date approaches, can be used simultaneously to provide maximum insight during the review process.

EXHIBIT 6.3 A Sample Work Plan

	ACTIVITIES/TASKS	Phase 1	Phase 2	Phase 3	Phase 4	TOTAL
1	**Reading Proficiency**					
	Cost (direct $)	4,000	12,000	12,000	12,000	40,000
	Teaching Time (TT in hours)	144	432	432	432	1,440
	Pupil Time on Task (ToT in hours)	3,600	10,800	11,800	12,800	39,000
	ToT/TT (hours)	25.0	25.0	27.3	29.6	27.1
	Cost/TT ($/hour)	27.78	27.78	27.78	27.78	27.78
	Above Reading Norm (%)	70.0	75.0	79.0	82.0	
N	**Other Activities, etc.**					
	Total Work Hours	144	432	432	432	1,440
	Add Authorized Leave (hours)	36	36	36	36	144
	Total Paid Hours	180	468	468	468	1,584

Exhibit 6.3, *A Sample Work Plan*, identifies reading proficiency as an activity/task in grade four of a primary school. As noted, this work plan could be expanded to also incorporate additional activities and/or tasks, serving to mark grade four as a comprehensive center of performance responsibility.

Work time forms the basis of work plans. Work time can be calculated by hour, week, month or year. As it reflects time-on-task, work time embraces all forms of effort, regardless of payment concept, including that of staff, whether permanent, part-time or temporary, overtime hours, and time of contractors, if used. In contrast, paid time forms the basis of budgets. Thus, at the bottom of the sample work plan, these two different concepts are reconciled with the addition of a calculation of "authorized absences." This usually includes vacation leave, sick leave, holiday pay, etc.

As also demonstrated by the sample, work plans should incorporate targets and performance ratios, wherever possible. Indeed, unit measures, such as, unit cost, cost per unit, output per work hour or work hours per unit of output provide a strong foundation for work plans.

By promoting Personal Education Plans (PEP), educators recognized the value of encouraging students to take responsibility for their personal development and academic achievement.

> *Author's aside: Circa 1988, I became acquainted with the concept of student engagement as a consultant with the Mary Casey Foundation. At that time, the Foundation was assisting several school districts, including the City of Lawrence, Massachusetts, in multi-year efforts to improve the life chances of "at-risk" teen-age students. The "Lawrence Futures Program" featured tripartite performance contracts between student, parent and teacher.*

If PEPs include references to milestones and subject matter mastery targets, they certainly qualify as work plans. Engaging students in academic work planning cannot help but enhance their commitment to achieve subject-matter mastery targets. Such engagements confer collateral benefits in discipline and increased time-on-task mastery instruction—the key ingredients of effective schools. Encouraging and monitoring formal student engagements requires resource commitments, principally teacher time. To that end, budgetmakers should establish, and fund, *Student Work Plans* as a budgetary classification. More on this important point in Part Eight, *Implementation: Dynamic Monitoring.*

> ***Informed observers have noted that ineffective schools are marked by practices that reduce the time devoted to active instruction. Reportedly, effective time-on-task is significantly less than teachers report and the district prescribes. The budgetary implications of significant wastage in deploying this key educational resource are serious, as academic achievement is directly correlated with the time devoted to instruction.***

Choosing a preferred course of action requires comparisons of the impacts and benefits of alternatives. Considerations include 1) an evaluation of intrinsic merit, applying objective criteria, and 2) an evaluation concerning relative merit, that is, weighing ascribed benefits, variously specified, to identify the alternative providing the best available net return.

Alternatives chosen for consideration should relate to the problem definition and goals, otherwise, the resulting budget documentation will lack logical coherence. Aside from standard achievement and attainment data, it requires imagination and ingenuity to devise ways to compare the impacts and benefits of alternatives. In general, data on costs and work time are much easier to assemble than data on benefits. Use the best sources available. Consult the literature for help in applying various analytical techniques, such as, willingness to pay, cost/effectiveness, benefit/ cost, etc. which might help in the evaluation of alternatives.

Attempts to compare alternatives require the specification of presumed linkages between variables. For example, teaching is supposed to "cause" learning. The presumed linkage between teaching (measured by time, costs, or subject matter units) and student performance is undoubtedly the most important presumption, in educational practice, now, and in the past. But, there are others. In fact, educational practice is based on a number of presumptions about the cultivation of learning, such as, age grouping, grouping by ability, pupil/teacher ratios, educational attainments of teachers, teacher experience, etc. As another case in point, referring to the common practice of stratification within classes and between classes, expectations about the ability to learn, positive and negative, implicitly or explicitly expressed, are thought to have decisive effects on student motivation and behavior.

Rising to the level of conventional wisdom,. presumptions about linkage often gain purchase as important causative variables within school environments. The budgetary consequences of presumed linkages are very significant. As manifest perplexities about the ways and means of education persist, educators must be ever-ready challengers of conventional practice. No presumed linkage should be accepted at conventional value. Each must be subjected to rigorous evaluation, seeking to specify its impact as an independent variable on student performance.

One cannot gloss over the difficulties involved in the specification of linkages. Even with extensive research, linkages "known" to be beneficial will resist specification, leaving their contribution to student achievement undocumented, but still appreciated. Yet, no budgetmaker worthy of the craft can turn away from this work. If production functions are unknown, alternatives cannot be properly weighed by impacts and benefits.

In these cases, budgetmakers are advised to employ "action research," essentially an experimental approach, aimed at building up a base of valid knowledge for implementation in future budgets. (See Statement 7, *Alternatives.*).

Remember also that the "means of implementation" is best built up in the course of consideration. Alternatives that look good analytically may not be deemed practical to implementers. Involving potential implementers in the analysis of alternatives is a good way to avoid wasting time and resources on consideration of unrealistic solutions.

Statement 6, Budget

As they display the resource implications of proposed work plans, budget proposal should identify expenditure by performance classifications. (If desired, identification by commodities can be added by means of cross-classified "line item" exhibits.). Budget proposals should include a funding/financing plan (taxes, grants, service charges, loans, etc.). and a multi-year projection of program costs and revenues. Each year's projection should list estimated resources which equal or exceed the proposed expenditure. Multi-year projections help appropriation authorities to get some idea of the future implications of adopting proposed budgets. For an indicative, annotated example of a performance-oriented public budget, see *Appendix A, An Annotated Model Published Budget.*

Statement 7, Alternatives

Statements 5 and 6 present the preferred solution to the situation identified by Statement 1. As recommended, in the course of settling on a preferred approach, budgetmakers should consider alternative solutions. A statement concerning alternatives considered, but rejected, is valuable as it provides all concerned with an opportunity to examine the preferred solution in a context of approaches, and, perhaps, values other than those expressed, explicitly or implicitly, by the author(s) of the proposal in question. Ironically, in citing reasons for rejecting alternatives, Statement 7 serves to highlight the criteria applied to justify the adoption of the allocation, as recommended. Further, the citation of alternatives, deemed impractical at the time, may spark interest in research that might produce future programmatic initiatives.

Key Thoughts in Review

Identifying "controlling" variables, "good" education budgets have a diagnostic foundation, rooted in student perplexities (issues, problems and opportunities) which can be programmatically addressed.

The recommended formulation and documentation process addresses the following seven topics: 1) Rationale, 2) Goal(s), 3) Collaborators and Affected Parties, 4) Conditions of Performance, 5) Preferred Solution and Work Plan(s, 6) Budget, and. 7) Alternatives.

Goal statements should be time-bound, practical and measurable.

As the "means of implementation" should be built up during the budget formulation process, it is important to involve implementers in the analysis of alternatives.

---

7. Adoption

...describes options available to appropriation authorities for review and approval of allocations formulated and submitted by administrative and program officials.

By any measure, arriving at judgments about the intrinsic and relative merit of proposed allocations is a challenging task for educational authorities. By far, assessing relative merit will prove the most vexing.

The typical district school board member does not have the time, or personal resources, to do more than question the justifications underpinning the proposed budget. The pressure to refund the existing organization and its established programs, combined with time constraints, discourage school district board members from serious probing, *de novo*, even if they had time. Although these circumstances tend to circumscribe the breadth and depth of their review, the following steps can help appropriating authorities adopt budgets based on evidence and logic. .

First and foremost, educational authorities are well advised to require the application of objective tests of merit by their staffs during budget formulation and documentation, thereby reducing the subjectivity of judgment required during the adoption process. At minimum, they should be assured that proposed allocations have been subjected to tests of intrinsic and relative merit by the application of the tools and techniques listed in Exhibit 6.1, *Budget Formulation and Documentation.* After all, from the school board member's point of view, an ounce of prevention is worth a pound of cure!

Without doubt, this insistence on adequate staff work during the process of budget formulation and documentation, done to exacting standards of evidence and logic, is the best way to ensure that allocations, when adopted, after thoughtful review by appropriation authorities, have intrinsic and relative merit.

Once the review is underway, the following steps are recommended:

- Throughout reviews, maintain a steady focus on programmatic, as well as financial data. In this perspective, financial data takes on meaning when it is logically and efficaciously related to programmatic thrusts addressing student learning issues, problems and opportunities. Remember: the merit of a budget depends on:1) relationships between allocated resources *(the less the better)* and stated purposes and *2)* the comparative worth of those purposes *(the more the better.* Thus, good budget review primarily center attention on what is to be done (*output*), or achieved (*outcome/impact*), and secondarily on what is to be bought (*input*).

- To assess the *intrinsic* merit of proposed allocations, examine proposed allocations for evidence that the proposers applied the formal criteria listed in Exhibit 4.1. *Allocation Criteria*, specifically, service standards, performance ratios and models.

- To help reach judgments concerning *relative* merit, examine proposed allocations for evidence that the proposers applied investment return calculations and comparisons, and weighting and scoring procedures. Accountable school officials who weigh the merits of alternative investment opportunities gain valuable insights into estimated gains and losses associated with various educational strategies. With regard to relative merit, educational authorities can do no better than to require the application of the concepts of a) comparative investment yield, when practical, and b) comparative marginal productivity.

- Systematically inquire into applications of the concept of "diminishing returns." Most assuredly, opportunity "costs" are associated with every benefit accruing to every hour of student time-on-task assignments. No assignment is costless from the student's point of view. Given the overall limitation on in-school learning hours, the assignment of student time becomes the key allocation issue for educational authorities. Proposed deployments may, indeed, provide positive benefits, but, what else is true?

Concerns about relative productivity direct attention to opportunities for displacing goals and substituting means, thereby probing the marginal effects of transfers of student and staff time. By plotting the marginal productivity of different programmatic patterns, it is often possible to chip away at deployments without significant loss in student performance, making time available for other educational ventures offering increasing returns.

In sum, by requiring that objective criteria be applied to proposed allocations, appropriation authorities express an abiding interest to all concerned that they seek the most productive overall distribution of scarce resources.

Key Thoughts in Review

An ounce of prevention is worth a pound of cure. This axiom is the key to an efficacious adoption process. Anticipating an adoption process which pits proposed allocations against one another, educational authorities are well advised to exercise foresight by requiring the application of objective tests of merit during budget formulation and documentation, thereby reducing the subjective judgments required during in the adoption process.

To maximize their effectiveness, appropriating authorities should 1) focus on programmatic data, and 2) assess the *intrinsic* and relative merit of proposed allocations.

8. Implementation: Dynamic Monitoring

... describes the best way to ensure that student achievement and attainment match intentions.

Although goal attainment is the purpose of budgeting, the critical implementation phase of the process is all too often treated perfunctorily. Metaphorically, one may even say that implementation is a neglected stepchild of budgetary theory and practice. Without a strong monitoring phase, the budgeting process degenerates into estimating, spending and accounting rituals. More than any other phase of budgeting, it is the practice of formal, periodic performance reviews which invests a budget process with "managerial muscle."

Specifically, given the mission of public education, the efficacy of budget allocations, and the resources they provide, should be periodically assessed for their intended impact on student achievement and attainment.

When conducted dynamically, as recommended, monitoring procedures can result in productive periodic adjustments to specific work plans assigning teacher and student time-on-task, As noted above, given that public education is an organized process, the monitoring of student performance is inextricably tied to the monitoring of organizational performance. Consequently, discussions about the ways and means of budget implementation must respect this duality of effect.

Traditionally, school principals are charged with monitoring teacher effectiveness. This practice has been criticized as ineffective, resulting in "flat curves" of acceptable performance and few dismissals, due to the protection afforded by teacher tenure laws. Recognizing this weakness, in recent times, many state governments have broadened teacher effectiveness criteria to include student performance, in effect, making teachers potentially hostages of their students. Obviously, every performance evaluation approach has behavioral consequences. Otherwise, why bother! In this case, making teacher performance dependent on student performance is a serious and controversial step, as it tends to promote practices, such as, "teaching to tests" and, even worse, manipulated tests and results. In addition to producing undesirable consequences, and most perverse from the perspective of this essay, this path to teacher accountability undermines the utility of tests as diagnostic instruments shaping teacher and student work plans. (The concept of student work plans is explored in Part 4, *Budgetmaker's Toolbox,)*

Concluding these preliminary observations about implementation, discussions of performance monitoring serve to reemphasize the importance of budget classification, explored in Part 2, because implementation processes should be centered on accountability for key resource allocations, specifically, time-on-task.

Essentially, adopted budgets represent an act of faith by appropriating authorities—an attempt to shape the future in desired ways. As such, budgets for public education simultaneously authorize, direct and limit expenditure, thereby affecting official and staff behavior. Thus, it behooves educational authorities to forge strong causal connections between their intentions, if made transparent, and results, if also rendered transparent. In this critical endeavor, the spotlight inevitably falls on the institutional foundations of budget implementation.

As will be suggested, implementation can be addressed by using "tools" readily at hand, but not usually found "working hand-in-hand." In administrative terms, these "tools" are inter-related practices which require firm institutionalization. These determinants are:

- Effective articulation and use of performance information.

- An elaborate, flexible budget classification and coding scheme.

- Accounting procedures which facilitate the aggregation of non-monetary performance data, formally correlated with measures of effort and monetary data—effectively, some form of management accounting.

- Continuous management utilization of four inter-related instruments of budget implementation. These instruments include a) work plans, b) allotments, c) periodic formal performance reviews and d) timely corrective action.

Effective budgeting (efficacious attainment of performance objectives) is best assured by using an institutional framework integrating these determinants and implementation instruments , with accounting procedures providing the glue. As these determinants and instruments are mutually reinforcing, the absence or limp implementation of one reduces the effectiveness of the others.

When conducted as formal affairs, periodic performance reviews tend to stimulate desirable organizational behavior, as follows:

- Anticipation of formal, periodic performance reviews influences behavior in the intervals between reviews.

- Conduct of the review, itself, influences behavior as the participants reach understandings and agreements concerning actions to be taken by particular parties.

- Reviews promote collaboration among units upstream and downstream of the implementer in question which have the resources or responsibility to assist the implementer solve problems defined during review proceedings.

- The reviews stimulate accountable officials to initiate corrective action in those cases where failure to attain stated targets is likely.

Effective organizations attain stated goals. Efficient organizations attain stated goals at "minimum or lowest" cost or effort, relative terms which acquire meaning only through comparisons. Assessing the efficacy of any activity requires the development and maintenance of data, and data arrays, as follows:

- Efforts devoted to stated intentions, expressed in terms of expenditure and work-time.

- Results related to stated intentions, expressed in terms of output/outcome/impact indicators.

- Calculations dividing effort by results, or results by effort. (performance ratios)

- Additional measure(s) or ratio(s) based on a comparable situation to provide reference for evaluation of the subject ratio.

To be readily available for work plan formulation and the subsequent performance reviews, the required performance data must be 1) identified, and 2) recorded. As incurred, costs and work time must be associated with appropriate activities and/or tasks identified in work plans, then summarized at pertinent milestones. Similarly, output data must be recorded and summarized. Over time, using performance as a guide, accountable officials will be in a position to encourage the formulation of plans to improve the relative effectiveness, efficiency and economy of program operations. "Performance" is similar to the terms, "efficiency" and "effectiveness" in that it requires comparison to give it significance, or meaning. In the following abstract calculation, a variance is derived by subtracting an ideal, standard or target (intentions) from results, both stated in similar terms: These terms can be absolute numbers, or unit measures or other performance ratios:

Results
<u>(Ideal/Standard/Target)</u>
Variance

In addition to revealing the magnitude of variance, the subtraction will provide an indication of the direction of the variance in that the stated performance will equal (=), exceed (+) or fall short (-) of the stated ideal, standard or target.

EXHIBIT 8.1 Performance Review Specifications

Formal performance review procedures established by regulation.

Principals, teachers and program leaders (all who supervise the work of others) are to be provided with a forum for oral, written and visual presentations.

To provide presenters with a supportive audience, reviews are to be conducted by a committee whose members are selected for their ability to assist the accountable staff to attain stated targets.

To qualify as "dynamic," the reviews should be conducted "before-the-fact," that is, two-thirds of the way through the current reporting period. So timed, the reviewing officials have time to authorize "corrective action" in cases of impending failure of work supervisors (especially principals and teachers) to meet targets.

Review covers prior reporting period (results related to intentions), current reporting period (estimates related to intentions), and next recording period (projection of intentions).

Committee secretariat documents proceedings, reporting formally to accountable officials regarding status of targets and recommended corrective actions.

Performance reviews provide formal opportunities for Work Plan implementers to address the officials and unit supervisors influencing their ability to attain their goals, presenting a) results compared to intentions for the completed prior period, b) revised estimates of results related to intentions for the current period and c) projected intentions for the upcoming period. The projections also provide a solid basis for allotment requests and for cash management planning.

By design, reviews should be conducted by strategically constituted Performance Review Committees ***two-thirds of the way through the current reporting period.*** So timed, with two-thirds of the period completed, accountable staff (all those who supervise the work of others, including teachers) have sufficient experience to calculate revised estimates for the current period, conditioned on proposed action plans for the remaining one-third portion of the period. These timely reviews provide sequential opportunities to ensure goal attainment by encouraging, and/or authorizing timely corrective action in those cases where results are falling short of targets. At the two-thirds point, if the projected unfavorable variances are deemed significant, the accountable officials have time remaining in the period to authorize corrective action (adjusted staff deployments, changed procedures, etc.) to put the performance for the period "back on track." This recommendation about the timing of reviews and subsequent "corrective action" are what qualify this process as "dynamic."

As recommended, formal performance reviews provide all those who supervise the work of others, including, most crucially, teachers, with periodic opportunities to address their colleagues and superiors concerning student performance. Ideally these reviews should be "stand up" presentation, supported by visual aids, when appropriate. All presentations should reference the commitments registered in the current work plan, with significant variances indicated and explained.

As previously noted, student performance tends to be positively correlated with instructional duration and intensity. Variances between planned and actual time-on-task commitments require attention and prompt corrective action, as do negative variances traceable to shortfalls in goods and services due from central process agencies of the school district. Performance reviews also identify other "management" problems, such as, equipment failure, delays in equipment repair and plant maintenance lapses.

As indicated by Exhibit 8.1, these reviews should be treated as formal occasions, with the staff assigned to each activity/task granted appropriate time for presentations.

Work Plans require adjustment as the work proceeds. As dynamic documents, Work Plans should always register the latest current estimates of work time commitments and output delivery dates. Therefore, performance reviews provide an opportunity to assess progress, and, if necessary, adjust future work time allocations, and, perhaps, output delivery dates.

Immediately following the conduct of a performance review, the Committee Secretariat should prepare a draft report for the Committee's consideration. Addressing significant performance "shortfalls," this report should recommend corrective actions to be taken by the accountable program manager and the accountable officials of the units identified during the review as sources of assistance. In general form, performance reports should outline 1) performance to-date, 2) problems encountered, 3) recommended corrective actions and, 4) performance targets for the period to be covered by allotment requests, and 5) recommended allotment(s).

The identification of recommended "corrective action" is not always easy. The term itself is an abstraction covering a variety of types of action which might be appropriate in given situations. Not all performance problems are immediately solvable. Often, performance improvements are far easier to identify than to implement, especially prescriptions for remediation requiring cooperation from students and parents. I n many cases, the recommended corrective action is rather like a 'band-aid" rather than genuine problem resolution. Frequently, reviews pinpoint recurring performance problems—problems which require systemic changes in operating procedures and budgets. As emphasized, representatives of key centralized process units, are expected to participate in these periodic reviews to help principals, teachers and students remove the causes of recurring performance problems.

The arrangements for the development and monitoring of student Work Plans will necessarily vary with grades. In the elementary grades, class size is usually limited and the essential teacher-student-parent cooperation is easier to obtain and sustain. The situation in the secondary schools is significantly different, as the faculty is specialized, with several classes with different students. If the particular district has stable homeroom assignments of students and teachers, the homeroom teacher can organize and implement the development and monitoring of student Work Plans. Otherwise, the district must assign teachers to groups of students for this purpose.

As previously noted, and re-emphasized here at the closing of this essay., the time-on-task arrangements supporting the development and dynamic monitoring of student Work Plans require specific budgetary allotments to compensate the assigned staff, but can be expected to yield significant benefits in student achievement and attainment.

Requiring the sustained attention of the district's leadership, the organization and coordination requirements of a performance review system include:

- Appointment of Performance Review Committees.
- Designation of Committee chairperson and secretariat.
- Arrangements for time and place
- Timely notification to all participants.
- Provision of projection equipment.
- Provision for audience seating.
- Conduct of reviews
- Preparation of Review Committee Reports
- Corrective action facilitating target attainment

In sum, performance reviews expose the fallibility of plans, for whenever intentions are compared to results, variances are the rule. Consequently, programmatic shortfalls and missed deadlines are to be expected. Considering the inherent fallibility of plans, all participants in performance reviews should strive to maintain a positive, rather than punitive atmosphere—avoiding fault-finding and criticism in favor of problem-solving and corrective action.

Key Thoughts in Review

More than any other part of the budgeting repertoire, it is the institutionalization of formal performance reviews that invests a budget system with "managerial muscle."

To qualify as "dynamic," the reviews should be conducted "before-the-fact," that is, two-thirds of the way through the current reporting period. So timed, the reviewing officials have time to authorize "corrective action" in cases of impending failure of work supervisors (especially principals and teachers) to meet targets.

Work Plans require adjustment as the work proceeds. As dynamic documents, Work Plans should always register the latest current estimates of work time commitments and output delivery dates.

The efficacy of budget allocations, and the resources they provide, should be assessed for their impact on student achievement and attainment.

When conducted as formal, periodic affairs, performance reviews tend to foster desirable organizational behavior.

Performance review participants should avoid faultfinding and criticism in favor of problem-solving and corrective action.

9. A Concluding Note

Exhibit 5.1, *Budget Formulation and Documentation,* suggested topics for the formulation and documentation of solution-centered, results-oriented budgets. Reflecting the importance of requisite documentation, this closing note clarifies the rationale for this topology by listing its advantages:

- Increases the probability that proposed allocations are well considered, anchored in specified relationships between intentions and results.

- Stimulates productive budgetary thought by requiring 1) definition of issues, problems and opportunities, 2) goal specification 3) identification of collaborators and affected parties, 4) specification of performance conditions, 5) composition of work plan(s), 6) programmatic and budget details, and 7) disclosure of alternatives considered, but rejected. This topical sequence is especially effective in centering thought on the ways and means of implementation, embracing goal setting and the formulation of work plans.

- Encourages an iterative thought process. The inter-relatedness of the topics encourages budgetmakers to "go back and forth" among them, adding and amending as budget proposers develop the text of each topic. In this connection, the phrase, "the devil is in the details," points up the usefulness of shifting from the general to the particular, and then back again. By alternating levels of abstraction, this iterative process stirs the mind, sparking ideas, clues, cues, insights, scenarios, etc.

- Furnishes a format for composition of an appropriate interpretative budget narrative, including numeric displays. As the text is open to choice concerning the level of abstraction, numeric displays can be inserted in texts to provide selected levels of detail supporting generalizations. As a rule, no numeric displays should be inserted in text without interpretation.

- Provides a base of evidence and logic to support dynamic monitoring, facilitating the comparison of accumulating results against original intentions.

Adopting this formulation and documentation scheme may be expected to have a salubrious effect on the quality of budget documentation, promoting the use of evidence and logic in the development of proposed budget allocations. Requiring such documentation provides a strong basis for performance articulation and usage throughout the budget cycle.

The formulation of work plans by superintendents, principals, teachers and program leaders (all who supervise the work of others) is absolutely necessary for the conduct of periodic formal performance reviews. Adequate work plans incorporate performance indicators as targets. The requirement for the formulation of work plans by all who supervise the work of others encourages the identification and dynamic use of performance information. The essential elements of an adequate work plan are displayed in Exhibit 6.2, *A Work Plan Model*, accompanied by details concerning their formulation and use.

By promoting Personal Education Plans (PEP), educational authorities recognize the value of encouraging students to take responsibility for their personal development and academic achievement. If PEPs include references to milestones and subject matter mastery targets, they certainly qualify as work plans. Engaging students (and by implication, their parents) in academic work planning and monitoring cannot help but enhance commitments to achieve subject-matter mastery targets. Such engagements confer collateral benefits in discipline and increased time-on-task mastery instruction—the key ingredients of effective schools. Encouraging and monitoring formal student engagements requires resource commitments, principally teacher time. To that end, budgetmakers should establish, and fund, *Student Work Plans* as a budgetary classification.

And mark this well: Conducting periodic formal reviews of work plans formulated by all supervisors is the best way to validate performance indicators proving useful in budget formulation, adoption and implementation. Distinguished from the passive practice of after-the-fact reporting, the dynamic use of performance data serves to illuminate the conceptual problems and issues which bedevil the process of performance articulation and usage under the best of circumstances. To qualify as "dynamic," the reviews should be conducted "before-the-fact," that is, two-thirds of the way through the current reporting period. So timed, the reviewing officials have time to authorize "corrective action" in cases of impending failure of work supervisors (especially principals and teachers) to meet targets. Consequently, in addition to providing the entire performance articulation process with a compelling rationale, the active use of performance data during budget implementation encourages and supports desired organizational behavior.

In sum, this extended essay on the ways and means of budgeting strongly supports the common-sense conception that the public schools have "production functions." In this perspective, school organization and procedures make a difference. More to the point, effective schools can make a significant difference in the life chances of their students, shifting the "bell curve" of achievement and attainment to the right, regardless of the pernicious influence of socio-economic status on learning readiness and motivation. As asserted throughout this essay, the recommended budgetary thinking and action can help to clarify and carry out this vital mission.

Assessment Essay

At the beginning of *Budgetary Thought for School Officials,* readers were invited to crystallize their thinking about budgeting by drafting a Benchmark Essay responding to the normative question, "What is "good" budgeting?.

Now, at the conclusion of your study, you are invited to revisit the question by composing an Assessment Essay.

What is "Good" Budgeting?

_____
_____
_____,etc.

Then compare the two essays. This comparison will serve to illuminate and document the impact of the concepts and practices recommended by *Budgetary Thought for School Officials*.

Appendix A
An Annotated Model Published Budget

EXHIBIT A.1 Alpha Technical High School

1. COST CENTER	BUDGET
Auto/Aero/Power	1,200,000
Business	420,000
Construction	480,000
Electrical/Electronic	720,000
Graphic Arts	1,020,000
Health Services	240,000
Mechanical Trades	1,300,000
Services	620,000
Total	6,000,000

2. FUNDING PLAN	
State Aid	2,000,000
Industry and Business Grants.	4,500,000
Property Taxes	(500,000)
Total	6,000,000

3. ESTIMATED BENEFITS	
Personal Satisfaction	+ but ?
Diffusion of Knowledge	+ but ?
Broadened Options	+ but ?
NPV of Extra Income Per Student	85,140

4. RATIONALE. This budget funds 1500 students, 83% of total applicants, highest ratio in Tech history. See the Five-Year Forecast for data related to this problem. Emphasis on mathematics and reading is expected to enhance academic achievement next year. This expectation reflects the recommendations of a faculty study of the issues, problems and opportunities related to academic instruction and performance. The study report has been made available to students, parents and the public.

5. PERFORMANCE DATA. Estimated to improve this year, all four ratios are set higher for next year. The marginal cost of attaining targets is estimated at $100,000 in computer expense and extra counseling.

EXHIBIT A.2 Performance Data

LAST YEAR	THIS YEAR	INDICATOR	BUDGET
84	95	% Above Reading Norm	98
85	93	% Above Mathematics Norm	95
90	92	Attendance Ratio	95
85	90	Graduation Rate	95

Curriculum design is based on annual surveys of skill demand in the community, and alumni "feedback." Support for the School's dual objectives is displayed by the cross-classification.

6. CROSS-CLASSIFIED COST CENTERS

EXHIBIT A.3 Cost Centers Cross-Classified

COST CENTER	ACADEMIC ATTAINMENT	VOCATIONAL ATTAINMENT
Auto/Aero/Power	480,000	720,000
Business	170,000	250,000
Construction	190,000	290,000
Electric/Electronic	290,000	430,000
Graphic Arts	410,000	610,000
Health Services	100,000	140,000
Mechanical Trades	520,000	780.000
Services	250,000	370,000
Total	2,410,000	3,590,000

Number of Students	1,500	1,500
Unit Cost	$1,607	$2,393

7. ESTIMATED BENEFITS. Graduates are expected to add an estimated average of $10,000 to their annual income during the first 20 years after graduation. This incomes stream has a net present value (NPV) of $85,140, discounted at 10%. The public's investment in the average graduate is currently estimated at $16,000. After age 16, students contribute their time, measured by foregone earnings, estimated at an average of $10,000. Thus, the investment, private and public, in a technical education is estimated to total $26,000. Subtracting this investment from $85,140 yields a net present value of $59,140 attributable to the Technical High program. Additional benefits are listed. The notation "+ but?" indicates that these benefits are deemed positive, but are of unknown value.

8. MARGINAL PRODUCTIVITY. The academic attainment budget is up $100,000, balanced by a decrease in the budget for vocational attainment. In the opinion of the faculty, this shift will not. reduce their ability to reach the indicated targets.

9. FIVE-YEAR FORECAST. Holding unit costs constant, the budget may be expected to rise by $400,000 each year to accommodate enrollment for 1,800 students, the design capacity.

EXHIBIT A.4 Five-Year Forecast

	BUDGET	STUDENT ENROLLMENT
Budget Year	$6,000,000	1,500
Future Year Two	. 6,400,000	1,600
Future Year Three	. 6,800,000	1,700
Future Year Four	. 7,200,000	1,800
Future Year Five	7,200,000	1,800

Notes

The first data array, displaying allocations is the basic element of a budget document. In this "performance" budget, the investment is classified in terms denoting purpose, in this case, development of technical knowledge and skills. As shown by the model, the sum to be invested is decomposed into "cost centers," each of which is a summary of subsidiary, undisclosed costs classified by analytical rather than control codes. These subsidiary aggregations may involve more specific cost centers which will tote up details of expenditure, such as, teacher salaries, supplies, etc.

The second data array directs attention to the sources of financial support. Obviously, the total of this data array must equal the total of the proposed investments. In those cases where revenue exceeds the budget, the excess should be shown negatively, and the excess assigned to fund another budget.

The third data array provides information on the benefits to be produced by the proposed resource allocation. Ascribed benefits should equal or exceed the investment. In those cases where benefits cannot be monetized, one can indicate the tendency of the benefit, positive or negative, and the fact that its value is unknown, by using the following shorthand:

$$+ \text{ but ?, or } - \text{ but ?}$$

The fourth commentary refers to program rationale, the essential foundation of solution-centered, results-oriented budgets. It reflects consideration of the issues(s), problem(s) or opportunity (ies) addressed by the budget, and identifies performance targets. If too voluminous, the commentary may incorporate significant detail by reference footnotes.

Number five is a data array setting forth performance expectations for the upcoming year.

Budgetmakers use cross-classifications to explore the dimensions of an investment proposal, highlighting and emphasizing its linkages and multiple values. The distribution of a proposed budget to impact categories, displayed by array six, helps to isolate portions of a proposed allocation for studies of unit costs and marginal productivity.

The commentary on estimated benefits, number seven, provides insight into key program assumptions and calculations, setting the stage for discussion of investment returns. Although the cost center array does not display historical comparisons, it is sometimes useful to refer to current and prior year experience.

Array eight discloses the effect of applying the concept of goal displacement and means substitution to the existing pattern of allocations, searching for opportunities to shift, rather than add resources.

A multi-year forecast is the ninth and final element of the model budget. Multi-year projections alert interested and affected parties to the future implications of adopting the budget, as proposed.

Appendix B
Per-Pupil Costs Related to School Size

The selective study of unit costs can reward budgetmakers with insights into the intrinsic and relative merit of allocations. For example, consider the scattergram below. It plots average per pupil costs against enrollment in sa district of 45 elementary schools. It directs attention to two situations that merit investigation. First, smaller schools tend to have significantly higher unit costs than larger schools, suggesting that larger schools yield economies of scale. Second, two schools of approximately the same size that have radically different per-pupil costs. The cause(s) of this difference bears investigation.

EXHIBIT B.1 An Illustrative Scattergram

```
Cost
Per
Pupil
2,600                            |
2,500                   O        |
2,400      O                     |
2,300         O    O             |
2,200                            |
2,100         OO   O             |
2,000              O             |
1,900              O             | O    O
1,800      O  OO   OO   O        | O    O
1,700         O    OO   O        | OO   OO
      _____|_____
1,600         O                  | O    OO
1,500              O             | OO   O    O
1,400              O             | OO        O
1,300                            | O    O    OO
1.200         O                  |
1,100                            |
      _____
       0  100  200  300  400  500  600 700 800 900
              Number of Pupils Per School
```

Inspecting the scattergram, one can visualize a trend line running through the plotted paired variables, representing the main tendency of the data. If drawn, it will clearly slope downward from left to the right. The linear equation for the "line-of-best fit" is $y = -.87x + 2,217$. The coefficient of correlation is $-.57$.

The matrix below summarizes the distribution of student unit costs by school size. Note that the scattergram is divided into quadrants, using average school size (464) and average student unit cost ($1,688) as dividers. The matrix displays the number of schools falling into each quadrant.

EXHIBIT B.2 An Illustrative Matrix

	Unit Cost		
Enrollment	**Low**	**High**	**Total**
Low	4	19	23
High	14	8	22
Total	18	27	45

A caution is in order. As calculations, per pupil costs employ the student as an unmodified "output" indicator. Ideally, pupil cost calculations should be fused with student performance to shed light on fundamental issues of educational investment. Therefore, school officials seriously interested in applying unit measures must move beyond per pupil costs to establish their relationship to student achievement and attainment, no mean task.

Appendix C
An Indicative Illustration of Modeling Procedures

The modeling process begins with the identification of "causal" variables, that is, factors in teaching/learning situations which are thought to 1) address significant perplexities, and 2) produce desired results. This diagnostic effort serves to center attention on significant issues, problems and opportunities. Consideration of relevant perplexities puts a variety of viewpoints to work. Indeed, the modeling process offers opportunities for constructive participation, not only by staff and school leaders, but by students and parents, as well. It is likely that teachers and students, will appreciate an opportunity to contribute to a modeling effort. By exploiting existing data sources, or by assembling special data samples, budgetmakers can employ correlation procedures to assess the impact of selected variables. As an example, let's select third grade reading competency as our perplexing situation. Manifest differences in reading competency scores, within schools and between schools demonstrate that a variety of causal factors affecting achievement are at work in elementary school environments. Following a process of consultation, and a search of the relevant literature, our model builders settle on three variables, each of which is thought to be an agent of learning:

- Verbal facility of teachers, K-3 (VFT)
- Performance feedback, the frequency of testing and diagnostic follow-up (PF)
- Parental interest (PI)

Each of these variables will have a range of values for affected students, thus, are assumed to have different degrees of impact on our competency objective. Briefly described, it is hypothesized that higher incidence of teacher verbal facility results in higher student achievement than lower incidence. Obviously, the VFT variable will count only if several teachers are involved. Performance feedback (PF) is also thought to have a direct relationship to competency. Students who know where they stand with reference to formal learning expectations, and whose work is guided by such knowledge, are likely to do better than students lacking this support.

A direct relationship can be postulated for parental interest (PI), the more the better, as far as test scores are concerned. (Please note that there is probably a positive "feedback loop" between competency and parental interest, because success begets success, and interest. For simplicity's sake, our model omits feedback loops. Such loops are prominent features of dynamic models, however. Addressing the data problems of parental interest requires ingenuity, persistence and statistical savvy. One can visualize a scale of parental interest based on data drawn from various sources, such as, parental participation in school programs, demonstrations of homework assistance and supervision, staff assessments of parental interest based on experiences, and the responses to questionnaires on the subject administered to both parent and student. (The Colman Study used an encyclopedia in the home as evidence of parental interest.)

The sample calculation below assumes that each independent variable is measurable. Certainly, the verbal facility of teachers can be ascertained by testing. Performance feedback can be measured by noting the number and duration of teacher interactions with each student concerning performance, the time of teachers invested in providing corrective instructions, teacher-parent consultations, etc.

Having identified our variables and their presumed relationship to our objective, model builders are now ready to get specific. Exactly how much weight can be ascribed to each variable? To answer this question, we must determine how much of the variation in reading competency scores is attributable to each variable. This problem can be stated thusly:

$$C = W_1 (VFT) + W_2 (PI) + W_3 (PF)$$

> where:
> C = student competence
> VFT = verbal facility of teachers
> PI = parental interest
> PF = performance feedback
> W_1, W_2, W_3 = coefficients

EXHIBIT C.1 Correlation Data

Class	VFT* "X_1"	PI* "X_2"	PF* "X_3"	C** "Y"
A	5	5	5	90
B	5	3	5	80
C	3	3	3	70
D	3	1	3	60
E	3	3	3	50
F	1	4	3	40
G	1	2	1	30
H	1	1	1	20
I	1	1	1	10

* Influencing Variables scaled low (1) to high (5)
** Mean Test Score

Putting the equation in algebraic terms, a simplified sample calculation follows:

$$Y = 9.7(X_1) + 2.8(X_2) + 5.0(X_3) + 4.2$$
Also stated as
$$Y = 9.7(VFT) + 2.8(PI) + 5.0(PF) + 4.2$$
Coefficient of Correlation, $R^2 = .91$

According to the results developed by the sample calculation, the Verbal Facility of Teachers" is a potent independent variable influencing student performance, measured by student achievements and attainments. "Performance Feedback" ranks second; "Parental Interest" ranked third.

Assuming data validity, school officials can apply modeling results to policies and procedures. If variables are found to be sufficiently influential, (suggested by significant coefficients of correlation) the budgetary implications are obvious. Certainly, budget allocations can foster and maintain strong feedback procedures. The intensity of parental interest can also be positively affected by school policies and budget allocations supporting school-based events, consultations, outreach programs, etc. If the parental interest variable proves to have a significant relationship to competence, one can devise program strategies to deliberately increase parental interest, thus creating an opportunity, under controlled conditions, to learn more about this variable.

Assume for a moment that the verbal facility of teachers is found to have the strongest positive relationship to competency. This variable is very sensitive to recruitment and retention policies, pay, benefits, recognition, etc., all factors within the control of a district's leadership. In other words, high verbal facility can be acquired by means of investment strategy. The same can be said for the other two variables, PI and PF. Both can be influenced in desired directions by school leaders who are willing to use such models to inform and influence their budgetary allocations.

On the other hand, should any of these variables prove to have little or no relationship to our competency variable, other variables may be inserted in the equation, and tested for significance, such as, teacher experience, teacher educational attainments, pupil/teacher ratios, student mobility, student motivation, funds spent on teaching supplies, academic expectations, student time-on-task, teaching techniques, etc. It is one of the great advantages of modeling that, once equations have been established, a model builder can insert a number of likely variables, searching for that combination of variables which reduces the amount of "unexplained" variation to a minimum.

While not minimizing the computational problems involved in modeling of the type discussed above, it is fair to say that problems of data availability and validity will prove the most vexing. Consider "parental interest," for example. Most educational authorities agree that parental interest influences student performance. Given its theoretical importance, this variable belongs in our model, yet we know that we will have considerable difficulty in its measurement. Measurement problems should not cause us to turn away from significant variables. After all, if we give up because of measurement difficulties, we will not be able to model at all, as many of the most significant variables in education are difficult to measure.

Appendix D
"Dropout" Reduction: An Indicative Illustration of Performance Budget Analysis and Documentation:

RATIONALE

In the last school year, ___ percentage of secondary school students enrolled on their 16th birthday did not graduate as expected. The personal, social and economic consequences of failing to complete high school need no documentation here. They justify special forms of intervention by public school authorities. Without special intervention, this measure of effectiveness is not expected to improve during the upcoming three year planning cycle.

The decision to "drop out" has precursors, which include outside-school (socioeconomic) and in-school variables. Relevant in-school markers are 1) weak acquisition of school-based skills of mathematics and language, 2) frequent absences, 3) failing grades, and 4) inappropriate behavior. The relative influence of these variables can be assessed by means of multivariate correlations, and directly addressed with targeted resource allocations. This approach also provides a strong basis for monitoring results.

Inadequate cognitive achievement in acquiring basic skills of mathematics and language is deemed to be the prime "cause" of withdrawals when students gain the withdrawal option. Because customary remedial efforts using increased teaching time and "focused" instruction works for many students, but not for potential "dropouts," the "cause" of low achievement (and withdrawal) is attributed to motivational deficiencies beyond the reach of the conventional approach.

The motivational variable is judged to be complex, partly stemming from poor past academic performance, coupled with inadequate understanding about the knowledge and skill demands of the economic system.

In addition to poor test scores, the dropout's indifferent school behavior serves both as an indicator and a "cause" of the withdrawal decision.

GOAL

Allowing for residential moves, sickness, etc., a graduation target is set at 90% or better. In the upcoming year, the District aims to narrow the District performance gap by increasing the graduation ratio from the 2xxx-xx benchmark of ___% to ___%.

COLLABORATORS AND AFFECTED PARTIES

As indicated, low academic achievement is strongly associated with dropping out. Of the _____ students dropping out of the 2xxx graduating class, ___ percent placed in the 4th Quartile in reading and mathematics, suggesting that low achievement in basic skills is a "cause" of withdrawal. Therefore, in framing this initiative, the 4th Quartile distribution of the 2xxx tests for 9th and 10th graders has been used to identify potential dropouts from their respective graduating classes. This group totals _____ students.

It is estimated that about ____%, or ____students, will respond to the conventional remedial program, and continue on to graduation. This leaves _____ potential dropouts. Of this group, ___ will participate in this proposed initiative in the 2xxx-xx.school year.

CONDITIONS OF PERFORMANCE

Test scores provide the best indicator of dropout potential. Therefore, the scores on frequent criterion-referenced tests will be used to benchmark and then measure progress.

In addition, as awareness concerning the knowledge and skills required in the workaday world is regarded as a positive program variable, work experience will be incorporated in the program design.

Although shown as an ineffective variable for this target group in conventional remedial programs, enhanced commitments of time-on-task devoted to reading and mathematics will be employed in conjunction with a multi-dimensional attack on student indifference. As indexes of motivation, attendance and truancy will be closely monitored as key performance measures.

At the point of evaluation, at the end of the coming year, an average positive test score shift of 25 percent is expected.

WORK PLAN.

To start in September, 2xxx-xx at one high school, this initiative features a teaching team working under the leadership of the principal. If successful, it will be expanded to three high schools next year, and all in following years. This enterprise embraces four production techniques: 1) tailored curricula (C), 2) intensive periods of instruction and practice in mathematics, reading and writing (TOT), 3) part-time employment (E) and 4) mentoring by business-world volunteers (M).

This programmatic solution to the "dropout" problem is described by the following equation:

$$A =. W_1C. + W_2TOT + W_3E + W_4M$$

A positive change in academic achievement, and ultimately, graduation, designated as attainment (A). is expected to result from the interaction of these four variables, although the relative weight (W) of each is unknown at this time.

About the Author

Edward Anthony Lehan, MA, University of Connecticut. In addition to serving in several senior local government posts, including chief executive and finance director, he is an author, teacher and consultant. His written work includes *Simplified Governmental Budgeting*, (Governmental Finance Officers Association, 1981). Additional publications by the Governmental Finance Officers Association include the monograph, "The Future of the Finance Directorate," 1977, and four articles at various times in its journal, "Government Finance." His major written work also includes *Budgetary Thought for School Officials*, (Cantabrigia) 1982; *Budgetmaking*, (St. Martin's Press) 1984; *Budgetary Thought for Budget Officers*, (Amazon) 2016; and *Managerial Thought for Public Finance Officers*, (Amazon) 2016.

His article, "Budget Appraisal—The Next Step in the Quest for Better Budgeting?" (Public Budgeting and Finance, Winter Issue. 1996) received the 1996 Jesse Burkhead Award. As co-author, he was honored with the Louis Brownlow Award for "Rebuilding a City: Modest Adventures in Hartford" (Public Management, 5/1967).

In addition to US cities, states and the federal government, his consulting engagements include the Governments of Jamaica, Thailand, Indonesia, Philippines, The Ukraine, Oman, Russia, Hungary, Poland, India, Turkmenistan and Jordan. Especially pertinent are engagements with the School Districts of Rochester, NY and Lawrence, MA.

www.ingramcontent.com/pod-product-compliance
Lightning Source LLC
Chambersburg PA
CBHW030013190526
45157CB00016B/2694